Why Black Men Don't Attend Church
and
How to Recover a Spirit That Attracts Them

EMERSON G. MILLER

Copyright © 2019 Emerson G. Miller.

All rights reserved. No part of this book may be reproduced, stored, or transmitted by any means—whether auditory, graphic, mechanical, or electronic—without written permission of the author, except in the case of brief excerpts used in critical articles and reviews. Unauthorized reproduction of any part of this work is illegal and is punishable by law.

ISBN: 978-1-4834-9852-2 (sc)
ISBN: 978-1-4834-9851-5 (e)

Because of the dynamic nature of the Internet, any web addresses or links contained in this book may have changed since publication and may no longer be valid. The views expressed in this work are solely those of the author and do not necessarily reflect the views of the publisher, and the publisher hereby disclaims any responsibility for them.

Any people depicted in stock imagery provided by Getty Images are models, and such images are being used for illustrative purposes only. Certain stock imagery © Getty Images.

Scriptures taken from the Holy Bible, New International Version®, NIV®. Copyright © 1973, 1978, 1984, 2011 by Biblica, Inc.™ Used by permission of Zondervan. All rights reserved worldwide. www.zondervan.com The "NIV" and "New International Version" are trademarks registered in the United States Patent and Trademark Office by Biblica, Inc.™

Lulu Publishing Services rev. date: 3/11/2019

Contents

Chapter I	Theories	1
Chapter II	The Black Church	13
Chapter III	The Research Plan	23
Chapter IV	Males Are Missing in The Church	29
Chapter V	Most Black Men Don't Go to Church	31
Chapter VI	Why Black Men Don't Attend Church?	35
Chapter VII	Church is Good for Men and Men are Good for Church	53
Chapter VIII	Black Men Join Liberation Churches, Mega Churches or The Nation of Islam	61
Chapter IX	What Black Men Need	67

Dedication

This book is dedicated to my son Jonathan. Having a son like him has been one of the greatest gifts in my life. He has been my traveling companion, teammate on the basketball court, someone to bounce things off and an excellent conversationalist. I will never forget how he always protected his younger sister Leah.

Acknowledgements

"All writing comes by the grace of God."
Ralph Waldo Emerson

It is to God that I give all praise and honor for not only the words, but the references, creativity, determination, and desire to complete this book. Special thanks to my friend and colleague Dr. Calvin Tait whose suggestion that I turn my workshop into a book, served as the catalyst to get me to take pen in hand, actually I put my hands on my keyboard, and begin. And last, but not least, I thank my wife, Patricia, who is the love of my life, my main source of encouragement, help in the time of need, and my personal editor.

Introduction

There is no doubt in the minds of any observant person that the church is devoid of men. The reasons for the male gender absence are numerous and almost unlimited. There is enough blame to go around as to why men don't attend church, however blame does not improve the state of black men and the church, neither does it bring about the change needed to attract men to our houses of worship. Having served as a pastor, university professor, social worker, substance abuse treatment program administrator, and psychotherapist, let me assure you there is no simple answer or quick fix for the missing men in the churches.

This book addresses the reasons men say they don't attend church, however, the majority of the observations and comments are empirically verified. Historically speaking, black men were church goers. In earlier generations, black men were much more involved in the church, and their religious faith bolstered their commitment to families and neighborhoods. In recent years one or two things have taken place, either men have failed the church, or the church has failed black men. Research reveals that church growth is greatest among congregations with healthy male participation. Churchgoers are more likely to be married and express a higher level of satisfaction with life. Religion significantly affects the level of an individual's happiness and overall sense of security.

We need to call the church back to men by addressing their needs. Men are looking for relevance and have been complaining for years that the church is not relevant to them. A recent survey showed that 92% of churchgoing men have never heard a sermon on the subject of work. Men want to be involved in a cause greater than themselves. Men want to be successful. Men want to be challenged. Men are looking for leaders and want to be leaders. Men are looking for brothers. Black men are looking to heal the father wound.

The book addresses how the church can develop a spirit to meet the above listed needs of black men. In addition, the church needs to develop a healthy masculine spirit in the church, develop into students of men, make the church more man friendly, and practice the art of friendship evangelism.

How We Got Here

This topic is appropriate for me because I find it to be interesting, fascinating, worthy of note and informative. I have previously investigated this topic, but would like to perform more in-depth, quality, doctoral level research and learn more about how to rectify what causes Black men's absences from church. Since I am an African American male this topic is very personal to me. I want to help people, especially African American males to maximize their relationship with God. I have spent the better part of my life servings as a pastor, an evangelist, a school administrator, a director of an alcohol and drug treatment program, a college professor, and a psychotherapist primarily in the African American community. In my practice of psychotherapy, I worked with Black boys, many of whom had no positive father figure in their homes. I have concluded that if we (human effort cooperating with God's power) save a man then we could save his family and his community as well. When I read Kunjufu's (1997, p. 29) assertion that "While 75 percent of the mosque is male, 75 percent of the Black church is female," this caused me to ask the question, what is the Nation of Islam doing to attract Black men that the church is not doing? Kunjufu's statement motivated me to become immersed in the subject, conduct significant research, present workshops, and eventually write this book.

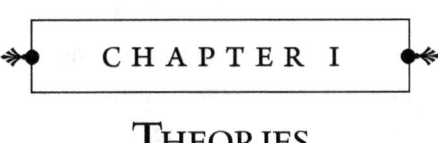

CHAPTER I

THEORIES

Women are Made for the Church and the Church is Made for Women

Noticeably a fascinating topic with innumerable important connotations, the phenomenon of women outnumbering men at church has been unrelenting to the point where the attention of many scholarly minds all seeks to unravel the complicated reasons for it. Scholars of religion have long known that women are more religious than men but propose divergent reasons for the underlying difference (Leffingwell, 2012; Stark, 2002; Walter and Davie, 1998). There are several theories that attempt to explain the disparity in religiosity between males and females. The literature review divides available research into two general areas: those that deem the gender disparity to derive more from the uniqueness of women (regard them more suitable for the Church) and those that ascribe it more to qualities of the Church (regarding it suitable for women). Jointly these two assortments envelop diverse theories.

Theoretical Outline
Part 1: Women Are More Suitable for the Church

Psychological Theories

Numerous psychological theories attribute a woman's proclivity for attending church to those characteristics that distinguish her from her male counterpart. Research has cited several differences between men and women. Women are more prone to feelings of guilt and anxiety therefore women are more likely to seek forgiveness from God. Warr and Ellison (2000) used data from a 1996 Texas Poll in which 1,006 respondents were interviewed about crime and other social issues. The analysis concluded that fear of crime is predominantly a female concern, but men are highly susceptible to altruistic fear when it comes to their wives and children. Buchko (2004) indicated that college women experience a strong spiritual relational component to their religious faiths than college men. That is, they daily encounter God through prayer, seek direction from religious advisors or teaching when coping with personal problems, feel assured that God is present and functioning in their lives, obtain comfort and self-assurance from faith, and express feelings of commitment to and admiration for God. Using the American General Social Surveys and the World Values Survey, Miller and Stark (2002) analyzed gender differences in religious beliefs and concluded that men appear to have a harder time listening and sitting still and are more aggressive and adventurous. Similarly, women are more likely to be dependent, nurturing, people-oriented, compliant, socially sensitive, responsive, and other traits that generally make them more relational compared to men who are more often independent, goal-driven, emotionally inexpressive, task and object oriented, focused on justice, and controlling—all of which leads them to value accomplishment more than interpersonal connections.

Gender orientation

Research that endorse psychological theories has unveiled at least two significant links that use distinctive gender differences as evidence that women are more likely to attend church simply because they are more suitable for it. This first one elucidates that church attendance is essentially based more on the gender orientation of individuals (in other words, whether they exhibit more "feminine" or "masculine" traits) than on their biological sex; determining that more feminine people have a greater desirability toward attending church services. That is, men and women who score higher on indices of femininity tend to be more religiously committed than men and women who score higher on indices of masculine gender role orientation. Attributes like empathy, nurturance, warmth, generosity, sympathetic, sensitive to the needs of others, understanding, compassion, tender and kindness to enemies have related to greater levels of religiosity which includes church attendance (Miller and Stark). Similarly, Sherkat (2002) concluded that heterosexual females and homosexual males are far more religious than heterosexual males or homosexual females.

Risk-taking

Directly related to gender orientation perspectives is risk-aversion theory. The theory hypothesizes that gender disparities in religiosity are a result of men's greater penchant to take risks, and that infinitesimal religiosity is like other high-risk behaviors normally associated with youthfulness (Miller and Stark; Roth and Kroll, 2007). The line of reasoning suggests that because women find taking risks objectionable, they prefer to engage in religious activities to make certain that they will be rewarded in the hereafter. On the other hand, men are more likely to take risks, and this extends to other risky behaviors such as drugs, crime, and delinquency (Ellis, Hoskin, and Ratnasingam, 2016; Stark, 2002). Some theorize that discarding the teachings of God and denying that He exists is risky behavior preferred for the sake of getting instant gratification through an ungodly lifestyle (Miller and Stark, 2002). Thus, men are more likely to be irreligious knowing that they risk divine retribution after death. Research using risk preference theory has not successfully distinguished those who identify a risk to irreligiousness from those who do not (Roth and Kroll, 2007).

Gender Role Theories

The previous theories described the concept that women attend church because of who they are, this second group of theories based on women being fashioned for church focuses keenly on what women do to determine how their roles in society could affect their predisposition to attend church. Several theories describe gender roles to explain why women are more attracted to church than men. The ideologies of separate spheres and secularization will be investigated to ascertain how gender roles may transmit to church attendance.

Structural location

One dimension of structural location that may influence the relationship between religiosity and attitudes is gender (Frost and Edgell, 2017). In the 1960s, it seemed apparent that in a gendered social division of labor women's higher religious devotion reflected both their freedom from the constraints of wage labor and their role as nurturer in the family. Women's chief responsibility for childrearing and family interests gave them more time for religious activity (DeVause and McAllister, 1987). Sullins (2006) has pointed out that time spent working simply lowers men's opportunity for religious involvement. If familial roles affect church attendance, then women who enter the labor force should become less attached to religion and therefore attend church less (Aune, 2008). However, such an association is not easy to unearth in large part since studies continually show similar levels of religiosity between working and non-working women (Walter and Davie, 1998). Evidence reveals that as more women enter the workforce, a smaller amount attend church (Aune, 2008; Francis 1997).

DeVaus and McAllister (1987) even found that women who work full-time are less religious than women who are full-time housewives; and that the religious practices of women in the workforce is very comparable to that of men in the workforce, although women who work full-time in fact attend church less than men who work full-time. Studies indicate that children in the family encourage church attendance for both parents (DeVause and McAllister, 1987). Even the factor of having children does not cause the father to rival the mother in church attendance (Barna Research Group, 2007). Conversely, among all categories studied, the jobless males display the least devoutness.

Secularization

Many researchers explored how church attendance rates are affected by mounting secularization. Secularization refers to the process whereby that which is sacred loses its significance and can occur on several levels: societal, individual, and within a religion itself (Casanova, 2006; Pace, 2017). Secularization theorists regard economic growth and the rise of economic modernity as central triggers for religious change that lead to a decline in church attendance (Hirschle, 2013). There are insufficient quantitative data covering the transition from traditional to modern societies that differentiate churchgoing by gender but what exists suggests that as societies became industrialized, women became dominant in church attendance and men's attendance decreased (DeVause, 1984). Women are central to patterns of religious change in the West. Quantitative studies of the United States, United Kingdom and Australia reveal that the more hours women spend in paid work; the less likely they are to attend church regularly (DeVaus and McAllister, 1987). With employment opportunities for women, the past century has changed in their favor as they enter what was formerly man's preferred space, the workforce (Aune, 2008).

A typology having three parts or members has been proposed by Woodhead (2005). Firstly, the women who engage in traditional roles as wives and mothers are immune from the effects of secularizing and retain a conventional church and family focused religiosity. Secondly, women who work outside the home and engage in domestic responsibilities when they get home will adopt forms of spirituality that accommodate for the stresses of juggling between two realities. The last representation is work centered women who are least likely to be concerned with Christianity; their religiosity resembles that of men. This model may not separate into three distinct parts and may not apply to all women. The model may work better as a continuum rather than as three diverse positions.

Whenever nontraditional behavior occurs where women trade or merge traditional roles in the private sphere (home) for those within the public sphere, church attendance will decline sharply as it has since the liberation movements of the past (Aune, 2008). Secularization theory describes what both genders do when adults operate in their traditionally assigned spheres; they are more likely to attend church than their secular counterparts.

Deprivation Theories

This third and final theory concerning women being more suitable for the church examines how women use the church as a basis of empowerment to adjust to the deprivation they experience in relation to men within almost every aspect of life. The research in this assortment of deprivation theories argues that women respond to such disparity by pursuing solace and confirmation in the church. Deprivation theorists argue that deprivation of different kinds leads to or encourages religiosity (Soares, 2016). Deprivation may be defined as a situation in which an individual is not able to realize one or several needs. Women in society have lower status in almost every aspect of life. Women are socialized to have a greater dependence on others through either learned helplessness or genuine need (Miller and Stark, 2002). Additionally, women face other difficulties especially because of their marked roles in society, such as pronounced economic need (Walter and Davie, 1998), further difficulty getting involved in the workforce (Miller and Stark, 2002), dearth of leadership positions, lack of an inspired voice in society, and lower political status (Miller and Stark, 2002).

Empowerment

Women face life and death situations such as pregnancy, labor and delivery which make them extra cognizant of their own mortality. Religious involvement promotes health and diminishes mortality by providing social integration within the family and the community, synchronizing health behavior, and assuaging the detrimental effects of daily stressors. Guilt is a dominant feature of women's experience and thereby drives them to church to seek forgiveness and acceptance because God is full of grace and compassion (Walter and Davie, 1998). Women tend to be more open about sharing personal problems and are more relational than men (Gallup, 2002); research shows a higher proportion of women than men say they have a best friend in their congregation. Thus, the female fellowship in the church environment empowers them even though the men in leadership positions received the recognition and admiration. Women can easily meet their need for connection and affiliation by attending church simply because it provides a place for relationships and security as opposed to independence and individuality.

Research reveals that in places without strong social safety nets to provide people with opportunities for upward mobility, people are more likely to rely on religion for comfort. As contradictory as it may seem, when someone is suffering it may console him or her to think that the end of the world is near, and that God will bring it to a close and reward the faithful with everlasting joy (Rees, 2009). Along these lines, an interconnected form of empowerment deals with the many issues stemming from patriarchal societies that consider men to be more prized than women. As with economic liability, lower social standing exhorts women to find not only temporary comfort in the church but also ways of moving up to a more valued position (Miller and Stark, 2002). The Bible teaches that God is no respecter of persons and that all human beings are equally loved by God because they are all his children. Additionally, Scripture thoroughly focuses on God's special care for those relegated to the lower strata of society like the exodus and the deliverance of God's people from slavery. Church venues often value the special qualities women bring to the church i.e. warm-heartedness, tenderness, feelings, and intuition which give women power that is denied in the larger society. Aune (2008) posits that these qualities that women possess repeatedly help them to realize otherwise difficult to obtain leadership responsibilities. Research shows that adhering to the Scriptural image of a male God actually encourage men to heed women's admonition to be better husbands, fathers and servant leaders (Aune, 2008; Coats, 2009); her submission therefore rewards her and her family by elevating the requirements for her husband's dedication to family.

The view of a male God has not been left unchallenged (Christ and Plaskow, 2016). Feminist theologians indicate a male God is a stumbling block to equality, harmful to the cause of human equality, oppressive, and all but inclusive (Goldenberg, 1979; Hampson, 1990; McIntosh, 2007; Nordling, 2005), yet, feminist theology remains on the periphery of mainstream academic and Christian circles. E. Margaret Howe, one of the leading feminist theologians today, observed that this idea of a male God is largely based on Old Testament descriptions that represents God as "Father," and disregards the Scriptures which characterize God as "Mother." The Lord is described as a nursing mother (Isaiah 49:15), midwife (Psalm 22:9-10), and a female homemaker (Psalm 123:2). Howe says the sexuality of God has repeatedly been underscored rather than His personhood. But we are in the sphere of mythology when we conceptualize God as male, rather than female, just as we would be if we regard him to be female rather than male. The being of God exceeds the confines of sexuality (Howe, 1979). Until feminist theology is proved important enough to compete with the overriding male metaphors supported by male-controlled privilege, realms of history and years of custom, then women will continue to feel devalued and dismissed in Christian culture (Bacon, 2012).

Empowerment and Black women

Elucidations of this inordinate sense of religiosity among women are not very persuasive when applied to Black women. Religiosity and devoutness have consistently surfaced as critical facets of Black women's efforts to account for, understand, unravel and deal with adversity (Bacchus and Holley, 2005). The experience of being discounted, oppressed, and subjugated by a male directed clergy has forced Black women to utilize multifaceted ways to position themselves within both the church and the broader world. Historically, African American women in the United States helped, created and shaped diverse and crucial models of leadership and community organization (Gilkes, 2001). Women's guilds that are controlled, organized, and structured by women have played a dominant role in the organization and maintenance of the outreach ministries of the Black church. The distinct role of Black women in service positions in the church may be the result of male central practices which preclude women's participation in other positions of leadership within the church. A second interpretation is that Black women may express their spiritual point of view in terms of perceptible efforts to alleviate social disparities by enhancing or involving themselves in social service programs. Historically, Black women have employed the essential doctrines of Christianity as the basis for offering pervasive challenges to unjust and degrading social conditions.

By means of a multi-method approach (quantitative and qualitative analyses), Mattis (2002) discovered a range of strategies used by Black women in their endeavors to modify unfavorable experiences and make them meaningful. Those strategies included accepting reality, confronting and rising above limitations, turning things over to God, identifying existential investigations and life lessons, comprehending purpose and destiny, and accomplishing growth. Utilizing these strategies, Black women construe the events which they encounter, and come to conclusions about what comprises a suitable coping response.

Part 2: Church Is Suitable for Women

Feminization Theories

The model of the Black church sprang from the white church to which African Americans were subjected and sometimes involuntarily compelled to attend during the early years in America. The early Black church only had one form of Christianity after which to replica itself, the white church. It was not until African Americans received their freedom and began mimicking the institutions of the white majority that sexual equality became an issue. The pattern of a largely female audience in the Black church started in the late nineteenth century (Lincoln and Mamiya, 1990). Research attributes women's church attendance primarily to the way women are made, another complete field of research takes into account particular church distinctiveness to be the decisive factor in unbalanced gender contribution (Edgell, 2013).

Christianity began to set in motion changes in the church as early as the reformation, instituting a focus on individualism that involved modifying the language from Latin to the everyday language of the people and changing the music from convoluted choir songs to simple hymns. The laity assumed more control over the liturgy and style of worship. The major expression of religion changed from exact specialized performance of the ceremony of the Mass to an individual expressive response to the person of Jesus. Protestants in the eighteenth century began to shift away from the God who is judgmental toward a loving nurturing God. The emphasis was shifted from formality to inner piety (Ahlstrom, 1972). Such doctrinal shifts gradually attracted more women and repelled men (Field, 1993). Church has continuously changed between periods of majority femininity and sizeable masculinity. Subsequently, Eldredge (2001) objected to the feminized church by challenging men to assume their rightful place by behaving the way God created them.

Women remain the majority in most Christian churches despite masculine movements. What was once a husband and wife faith turned out to be relegated primarily to the private sphere (home), thus feminine qualities like issues of home, family, and relational values began to dominate. Eventually, women turned out to be so pervasive in the church that they became the most important benefactors and transmitters of Christianity. Christian women simply shaped the church to match their needs and produced the over-romanticism and emotionalism of religion. Christianity lost all power to engage critically or intelligently with modern socioeconomic developments (Eldredge, 2001).

Even though the church is still led almost totally by men, the faith became increasingly inundated with women's values (Fenn, 2003), such that even its depiction of God took on more feminine characteristics that centered around relationships based on love, trust, and care instead of the more active masculine traits like judging, directing, and leading. The approach to worship reflected feminine themes (i.e. interaction, relationship, and intimacy). Thus, feminine characteristics came to be more acceptable than male qualities (Fenn, 2003).

Men are absent

For every reason identified for why women are attracted to church those same reasons reflect why men don't attend. The church makes it difficult for men to be themselves (Eldredge, 2001). Men focus on applying intangible ethical principles to concrete situations; women make moral decisions based on relationships and interpersonal agreements (Bryant, 2007). Men are independent; therefore, they have a problem with relinquishing their pride and submitting themselves to a male God. Men are less involved in church due to secularization. Secularization is defined as the process by which sectors of society and culture are removed from the domination of religious institutions and symbols (Berger, 1967; Martin, 2017).

Women are steadily becoming less involved in religion (Barna, 2015; Woodhead, 2005). A study by the Pew Research Center (2018) has discovered that while Black men are not as religious as Black women, they are more religious than white women and white men. Barna related that the declining support of women may make ministries respond by increasing the male-friendliness of the proceedings and pressure men to upgrade their church involvement.

CHAPTER II

THE BLACK CHURCH

To perceptibly understand the dynamics of why the church is suitable for women, the history of the African American people before and after emancipation must be examined. This information raises awareness of the conditions in society for African Americans. Historians and other scholars of the African American experience agree that the church has played a vital role in African American life.

DuBois's work, *The Negro Church* (1903) was the first major sociological research project of the church that was based on empirical evidence. DuBois and his associates interviewed more than 1,000 young African Americans about their religious convictions, performances and ideas. DuBois's contribution to the study of the Negro Church was his historical contention about the viability and impact of African culture. The Black church is the only social institution which started in Africa and survived slavery. The church preserved the remnants of African tribal life and became after emancipation the core of Black social life (DuBois, 1903). Du Bois highlighted the partial independence and creativity of Black culture. This was a critical achievement in his day when normative presumptions of African cultural backwardness abounded (Evans, 2007). When Africans were transported to the new world, they were given instruction in the Christian religion. African slaves received wholeheartedly this feature of the Christian religion and, in doing so, recognized that those who taught them this religion did not always practice it themselves. Religious training was given to the slaves as early as 1695. The British Society for the Propagation of the Gospel in Foreign Parts was the primary agency in this undertaking (Comminey, 1999).

For countless African Americans, religion and spirituality have been an important part of their lives. They serve as the underpinning for African Americans' extensive history of a strong faith tradition (Gillum, 2009; McGee, 2017). Black religious conviction has provided fortitude to rise above the horror of slavery and the terror of Jim Crow. African religious tradition centers on oral traditions told in the form of stories that are routinely passed down from one generation to another. Akin to oral tradition in Africa, slave children were given instruction in Christianity by parents, family, or older slaves (Jones, 1842; Slavery and the Making of America, 2016). African religions stress ancestor adoration; the ancestors are revered for the reinforcement of the linkage of heritage and spiritual importance. Ceremonies in the Black church such as baptisms, christenings, and funerals give emphasis to the common bonds of kinship between those who have died, the existing, and the not yet born. Earliest African belief stressed the needed balance between one's group identity and duty as a member of a society and one's individual identity and responsibility. A person is noticeably defined as a vital part of a distinct community to which she/he belongs and in which she/he finds distinctiveness and significance. In Africa, the fortune of the individual was connected to the tribe or the group. In America, Black people were infrequently recognized or treated as separate distinct persons; they were typically dealt with as envoys of their race, as an exterior outcrop. Consequently, the cooperative sense of freedom has an internal African origin peculiarly reinforced by hostile social conventions imposed from outside on all African Americans as a caste (Lincoln and Mamiya, 1990; Wilmore, 1998).

The Black church can scarcely be understood apart from the social and historical framework of its foundation. The church became the sphere of influence for the expression, celebration, and uncovering of the Black collective will and identity (Higginbotham, 1993). The church was the place of personal courage and cooperative empowerment against the domineering white culture (McGee, 2017). Lincoln and Mamiya (1990) contended that religion was perhaps the greatest paradigm to cultural understanding, that culture was a mode of religion, and religion was the core of culture. The reality of bigotry and racism birthed this most effective institution in the lives of African Americans and provided an opportunity for African Americans to worship, assemble and organize for liberation. Often this organization during slavery offered sanctuary and refuge from a dehumanizing world experience, a place to strategize for insurrections, disseminate anti-slavery information, educate the slaves and hide fugitive slaves (Littlefield, 2005; Weisenfeld, 2015). For the slaves, the church was the only setting where they could exercise a measure of independence and self-rule (Lincoln and Mamiya, 1990). Many slaves who were permitted by their owners to attend revival services and camp meetings accepted the Baptist faith in record numbers. In resistance to immoral systems of oppression, Baptists preached the equality of all believers and the sovereignty of faith in local communities of the faithful. In this sense, for slaves, the Baptist message assured full humanity and democracy notwithstanding the constraints of the unchurched world (Pinn and Pinn, 2007). It has been documented that the reason why most Blacks joined the Baptist denomination was because of semblances between West African practices and Baptist rituals (Johnston, 1954). Additionally, the Baptist denomination also gave ardent support to Black clergy (Johnston, 1954). From the period of slavery to the Civil Rights Era, the Black church centered on empowerment and has progressively moved on a path toward freedom and equality. This practice continued through the Civil Rights movement of the 1960s, when momentous and notable economic and political gains were made (Lincoln and Mamiya, 1990). The church was and remains for the most part the most powerful institution for racial self-help in the African American community (Harris, 2001; Martin, 2013; West and Glaude, 2003). During the mid to late 19th century, a period of increased institutional building in the aftermath of slavery, Black churches became the focus of Black life, operating not only as places of worship for congregants but also as the catalyst behind schools, business enterprises, intelligibility, politics, and recreation. Urban churches, in many instances, offered a range of outreach services, urging congregants to help reform prison inmates, visit hospitals, and provide food and clothing for the impoverished (Harris, 2001; Lincoln and Mamiya, 1990). Schools were among the first enterprises to be supported by churches. Formally detached from the white churches following the Civil War, the Black churches worked with the assistance of Northern philanthropists and their churches to set up schools throughout the South (Hall, 1997). The support of churches in educational endeavors was so strong that members of the congregation pooled together their small resources to pay teachers' salaries, buy books, or rent extra space for class rooms. Others would be of assistance by accepting teachers into their homes since some of them could not afford housing on their own given their limited resources (Montgomery, 1993,).

The Black church is flexible and adaptable depending on the issues and social conditions of the point in time. To demonstrate the church's flexibility Lincoln and Mamiya (1990) presented six didactic models which affirm the flexibility of the Black church. Although they conversely relate, the church's actual practice is somewhere within the continuum. These models are merely frameworks; a church may carry out more than one model at a time.

1. The dialectic between priestly and prophetic
   Priestly and prophetic functions are performed by every Black church. Priestly functions entail activities that involve worship and the spirituality of the members, while the prophetic functions refer to social issues and community uplift. Some churches leaned more toward the priestly while others leaned toward the prophetic.

2. The dialectic between otherworldly versus this worldly
   Otherworldly refers to being heavenly minded at the expense of doing no earthly good. It is as if one can be too spiritual and therefore out of the world. On the other hand, worldly depict churches which

believe that the church should be concerned with social, economic, political and the collective well-being of the people.

3. The dialectic between universalism and particularism
Universalism implies that correct behavior can be defined and always applies, while particularism suggests that relationships, survival, dignity and respect come ahead of abstract social codes. This describes the unconditional love of the Christian message and the actuality and effect of racism in the mission of the Black church. The lived experience of African Americans causes some churches to lay emphasis on Black consciousness.

4. The dialectic between the communal and the privatistic
The communal churches minister and participate in every aspect of the lives of the membership including political, financial and societal; the privatistic churches are concerned with meeting only the religious needs of the members.

5. The dialectic between charismatic versus bureaucratic
This refers to the organizational structure of the church. The organizational structure tends to move toward charismatic (a person centered) as opposed to a bureaucratic which seems to be governed by a system to insure order and functionality.

6. The dialectic between resistance versus accommodation
This describes the churches' capability to preserve a level of self-help and fortitude while also socializing its members into the cultural norms and ideals of the populace. The persistent debate about whether the Black church has lost its activist role in the community is embedded in the historical resistance versus accommodation dialectic. The resistance stance positions the Black church for involvement in social justice and moral action, electoral and protest

politics, redress for social problems; the accommodation perspective thwarts these processes.

The dialectical models are significant because they give a panoramic picture of the role and function of the African American church as an institution concerned with religious, social, political and financial matters. These models are also helpful in identifying the type of church most likely to serve monetary functions in the community and why the church is responsive to contemporary social conditions. Prior to 1900 and beyond, Black churches experienced instant growth both numerically and structurally.

Black churches may be categorized with respect to whether they embody denominations which are independent and separate from whites (historic Black denominations), or whether they are associated with predominantly white denominations. Eighty percent of African Americans belong to historical Black denominations (Lincoln and Mamiya, 1990; Swatos, 1998). Among African American women, 62% are members of historically Black protestant churches, among men, 55% are members of historically Black churches (Pew Research Center Religious and Public Life Survey, 2009). Even Blacks who belong to mostly white, mainline Protestant denominations tend to assemble in predominately Black congregations per Lincoln and Mamiya (1990). Lincoln and Mamiya (1990) described the seven-major historic Black denominations: the African Methodist Episcopal (AME) Church; the African Methodist Episcopal Zion (AMEZ) Church; the Christian Methodist Episcopal (CME) Church; the National Baptist Convention, USA, Incorporated (NBC); the National Baptist Convention of America, Unincorporated (NBCA); the Progressive National Baptist Convention (PNBC); and the Church of God in Christ (COGIC), as comprising "the Black Church." Yet Blacks were also members of predominantly white denominations such as the Episcopal, Presbyterian, Congregational, United Methodist, United Church of Christ (Congregational Christian), Seventh-day Adventist and Roman Catholic churches. However, Lincoln and Mamiya decided to confine 'the Black Church,' to "those independent, historic, and entirely Black controlled denominations, which were founded after the Free African Society of 1787 and which formed the core of Black Christians." Since the publication of Lincoln and Mamiya's book, two new Black denominations have developed: The National Missionary Baptist Convention (NMBC) and the Full Gospel Baptist Church Fellowship (FGBCF). The FGBCF does not refer to itself as a denomination (BlackandChristian.com, 2017; The black church experience, 2009).

The civil rights movement and the Black church

A. Philip Randolph spearheaded a movement in the 1940s that served as the foundation of the future civil rights campaign. He organized and led the Brotherhood of Sleeping Car Porters, the first predominantly Black labor union (Williams, 2013). He threatened to march on Washington, D.C., to force President Franklin D. Roosevelt to issue an executive order making fair employment a reality for African Americans. Roosevelt reluctantly issued Executive Order 8802 in 1941 which was confined to the armed services. Racial discrimination was forbidden in the defense industries during World War II. Randolph and his followers then effectively coerced President Harry S. Truman to issue Executive Order 9981 in 1948 that ended segregation in the armed forces.

During the civil rights movement, the Black church became collectively involved to address justice, freedom and equality for all (Chandler, 2017). The Black church became the voice against social inequity, discrimination, unfairness and organized and financed protests (Lincoln and Mamiya, 1990). Throughout the push for social reform and political transformation, Black churches and their leaders came full circle and invigorated the traditional connection between Christianity and political activism. Community activism contributes to the church electing political candidates (Brown and Brown, 2003) and regular church attendance is associated with participation in political involvement and civic affairs. There are strong correlations between the degree of religious observance and political involvement; those reporting regular church attendance are a great deal more likely to vote.

The pastoral pedagogy and responsibilities changed emphasis and focused on the theological underpinning, ethical, and rationale for the movement (Lincoln and Mamiya, 1990). African American leaders were willing to make tremendous sacrifices for the betterment of the community. Dr. Martin Luther King, Jr. drew on the non-violent resistance stance of Gandhi and the Black theological perspective of freedom and justice to give impetus to the civil rights movement. By 1979 seventy-one percent of Black pastors reported that their churches participated in community development programs.

The role of women in the Black church

Historically, the role of Black women in the Christian religion has been diverse. In Africa, women gave guidance in the areas of medicine and religion. Slavery did not lessen the role of women in Black culture, and when freedom was achieved Black women repeatedly played a helpful role among their people. Thus, women sought to develop their own voice and pursue their own interests in an organization controlled by men (West and Glaude, 2003). They believed that the spiritual, social and intellectual salvation of millions of African American people hinged on their work. Women in the church were responsible for providing funding for various programs and running programs such as schools. African American women associated with the National Baptist Convention launched some 154 societies. Women were not allowed to serve in leadership positions in the Baptist Convention; they formed their own Woman's Convention however they were not allowed to use the term Convention. The National Baptist Convention consented to the organizing of the Woman's Auxiliary in 1900 (Hall, 1997). The term Auxiliary refers to a subordinate organization or group. For the women to play a larger part in the religious life of their churches, they often started women-only groups. Nannie Burroughs establishing "Women's Day" in Black Baptist churches in 1907 has spread to every predominantly Black congregation and to Black congregations within mainly white denominations. Burroughs decided on the fourth Sunday in July as the proposed

National Women's Day. Burroughs envisioned Women's Day as a day primarily for praising women and a magnificent opportunity for women to learn to speak for themselves (Gilkes, 2001). The main purpose of Women's Day was to uplift the women; to train them for leadership, to better prepare Black women for work within their communities and to teach them through genuine, organized, challenging speeches on how to get sizeable contributions for Foreign Missions.

In Black churches, women generally were not permitted to preach. One notable exception was Jarena Lee, born in February 1783 to free but poor Black parents. Jarena Lee was likely one of the first African American female preachers in America. After hearing a sermon by Richard Allen, the founder of the African Methodist Church (AME), Lee sought permission from Allen to preach. First, he refused, and then changed his mind, granting her permission to preach on an itinerary circuit and to hold prayer meetings in her own home (Lincoln and Mamiya, 1990; Mellowes, 2010). Frequently, Black women who desired to preach were forced to start independent churches or join white churches. A number of female leaders in this era raised the issue of women's ordination, only to be rejected by the male-controlled leadership. It was not until the late nineteenth century that female pastors were ordained in the AME Zion church. Mary Small was the first female elder to be ordained in 1897 (Collier-Thomas, 1998). The AME and CME Churches did not ordain women until the middle of the 20th century.

The number of Black female clergy members is around three percent nationally. The approval rate for women preachers is low. However, approval rate differed depending on denomination. Methodists were extremely positive compared to the negative assessment of Baptists and Pentecostals. The struggle for equality and acceptance in the Black church is ongoing and has developed into a form of Black feminism.

CHAPTER III

THE RESEARCH PLAN

Introduction

Chapter three describes the research methodology that was used in this study by specifically, outlining the research design, study area, study population, sampling procedure, data collection procedure, data analysis and research ethics and evaluation. The data was collected from African American males who were residents of South Bend, Indiana.

Qualitative Research

There are several definitions of qualitative research. According to Brink, et al (2017), the qualitative approach is a wide-ranging research method used to examine phenomena of social action and of which researchers do not have a clear understanding. A number of authors emphasize the research purpose and focus: Qualitative researchers seek to understand the meaning people have established, that is, how people make sense of their world and the connections they have in the world (Grove, et al, 2015; Merriam, 2009). Others emphasize an epistemological stance; unlike epistemology, epistemological reasoning does not seek universality or absoluteness; it is neither a normative, standardizing, nor a flawless discipline (Miller and Fredericks, 2002; Schmidt, 2001). It consists of an unremitting, innovative activity that is reintroduced time and again. Qualitative research is research using methods such as participant observation or case studies which result in an explanatory, narrative, descriptive account of a setting or practice. Qualitative research is a positioned activity that locates the observer in the world. It consists of a set of instructive, material practices that makes the world observable. These practices transmute the world. They turn the world into a series of depictions, including field notes, interviews, dialogues, photographs, recordings, and memorandums to the self. Qualitative research involves an interpretative, true-to-life approach to the world. This means that qualitative researchers study things in their natural settings, endeavoring to make sense of, or to understand, phenomena in terms of the connotations people bring to them (Denzin and Lincoln, 2005; Welman and Kruger, 1999).

For this study, the qualitative approach was used to provide accurate data for theological reflection (Linton and Mowat, 2006). The qualitative approach supported the exploratory nature of this study. According to Neuman (2006), in qualitative research, procedures are particular, and replication is very rare (Pembroke, 2011), and measures are created in an ad hoc manner and are often specific to the individual setting or researcher. In this study, the qualitative approach allowed the researcher to refer to data collected by interviewing men who did not attend church.

The Study Population

The target population refers to the subjects or participants from which data for the study is drawn (Grove, et al, 2015; Brink, et al, 2017). According to Neuman (2006), the population is also referred to as a pool; the researcher specifies the unit being sampled, the geographical location, and the temporal boundaries of the population (Waller, et al, 2018). Effective participant recruitment is an important aspect of conducting qualitative research (Namageyo-Funa, et al, 2014). The subject of this study was to seek to answer the question, "how can one evaluate why is it that so many Black men in South Bend, Indiana don't attend church?" Therefore, the target population of this study consisted of African American men who resided in South Bend, Indiana that did not attend church.

Sample Size

Adams and Schvaneveldt (1991) suggest that the size depends on the purpose of the study, design, data collection, and category of population available for the research problem. Therefore, the decision concerning sample size depends on the predictable thoughtful coverage of the phenomenon. Most scholars argue that the essential concept for sample size in qualitative studies is saturation (van Rijnsoever, 2017). Saturation is closely attached to a detailed methodology, and the term is inconsistently applied (Malterud, Siersmaa, and Guassora, 2016). Creswell (1998) recommends long interviews with up to 10 people for a phenomenological study, therefore, for this study a sample size of 10 was selected. The participants were ten men from various neighborhoods in South Bend, Indiana. The researcher visited barber shops, community centers, men's clothing stores, restaurants, and the shopping mall. All the men agreed to participate in the interview. After the consent form was signed the process involved a semi-structured interview with the participants. Each one had their own questionnaire and interview time.

Face-To-Face Interviews

This study employed the face-to face interview to take advantage of what Cohen, Manion and Morrison (2007) refer to as the likelihood for the interviewer to survey the surroundings and use nonverbal communication and visual aids to guide the data or information gathering process. It is important to have a well-trained interviewer that can adjust with the conversation, as the discussion may not flow exactly as specified in the questionnaire. Marshall (2016) lists several advantages of face-to-face interviews:

- Allow for more in-depth data collection and comprehensive understanding
- Body language and facial expressions are more clearly identified and understood
- The interviewer can probe for explanations of responses
- Stimulus material and visual aids can be used to support the interview
- Interview length can be considerably longer since the participant has a greater commitment to participate

Semi-Structured Interviews

The semi-structured questionnaire was used in face-to-face interviews with African American men. In each interview, the procedure began with the interviewer establishing rapport by introducing himself to the candidates. The researcher then assured the interviewee of confidentiality and discretion in maintaining anonymity and that the information provided would be used precisely for the research only. The researcher asked questions individually to the interviewees directly. The process was tape recorded in order to capture the thinking of the interviewees and avoid personal interpretation. The structured questionnaire enabled the interviewer to ask the participants the same questions in the same sequence (Kanak and Arslan, 2018). Added questions for clarity on the information provided by the interviewees were required when the responses were not clear.

At the end of the interview appreciation was offered for allowing the interaction to take place and for the participant's time and information provided. The participants were reassured that their comments would be kept private, their identities would not be made known, and the researcher was the only individual analyzing the responses and that these answers would be kept safely in a secure location.

Perspective of the Empirical Research

The research was driven by practical experience and not theories (Cartledge, 2003). Qualitative research is a methodology in which the data obtained is in the form of words and observations rather than numbers. The best way to gather information is to listen to the stories as told by the interviewees (Auerbach and Silverstein, 2003). Semi-structured interviews allow the researcher to ask open and closed ended questions by means of a questionnaire (Osmer, 2008). Questions were numbered and arranged in a systematic fashion. The study was built on uninterrupted interviews, direct observation and questioning procedures.

The strength of this method enabled the researcher to gain first-hand awareness of the experiences of Black men and their non-attendance in the Christian church. The interviews with the respondents gave the interviewer the opportunity to enquire further into their responses that were not clear and in the process scrutinized their body language and speech. The method required that the researcher recognize his own bias and ethics (Auerbach and Silverstein, 2003).

CHAPTER IV

MALES ARE MISSING IN THE CHURCH

This book investigated a pastoral issue that is prevalent in most Black churches in the United States of America; namely, the shortage of men in the congregation. It is a pastoral dilemma that is acutely real within the confines of all churches but more disproportionate in African American churches. Scholars have noted that women outnumber men on all indices of religiosity and spirituality including church attendance, belief and commitment (Barna Research Group, 2007; Day, 2008). According to Collett and Lizardo, (2009); Sullins, (2006), gender difference in church attendance is one of the most consistent findings in the sociology of religion. In past decades, new interest developed in explaining this gender difference, advancing a project that began in earnest in the 1960s (Sullins, 2006). Research shows, and evidence supports that the extent of African American males attending church is considerably less than females (Kunjufu, 1997; Lincoln and Mamiya, 1990; Taylor, Thornton and Chatters; Mattis, et al, 2004). The typical United States congregation attracts an adult assembly that is 44% female and 36% male (Barna Research Group, 2015), however the gender gap is more extensive in the Black church. The typical Black congregation is around 75% female and 25% male (Hodges, Rowland, and Isaac-Savage, 2016; Lincoln and Mamiya, 1990 cited in Kunjufu, 1997) although per the Pew Forum (2008), people of African ancestry were most likely than other ethnic groups to be part of a formal religion, with 85% being Christians.

Attendance at midweek services/activities seems to be the same for both African Americans and those of other ethnic groups. With few exceptions, 70 to 80 % of the participants are female. In addition, Christian universities are becoming convents. The typical Christian college in the United States enrolls almost two women for every man.

Consider that while 90 % of American men believe in God, just a little more than 83% profess to be Christians. The belief is there, but church attendance is seen as having little value. Fewer than 10 % of U.S. churches are able to establish or maintain a vibrant men's ministry (Barna, 2011).

The disparity in men's attendance in American churches has made them the focus of specialized ministry over the last two decades. Two of these ministries are the Promise Keepers and The Million Man March. Promise Keepers kicked off the men's movement in 1990 by challenging stadiums full of men and boys to fulfill their duties to God and their families. The Million Man March was a gathering of Black men held in Washington, D.C., on October 16, 1995.Under the leadership of Nation of Islam's Louis Farrakhan, Black men were challenged to unite in self-help and self-defense against economic and social ills plaguing the African American community.

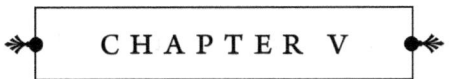

CHAPTER V

MOST BLACK MEN DON'T GO TO CHURCH

Historically speaking, Black men were church goers. In earlier generations, Black men were much more involved in the church, and their religious faith bolstered their commitment to families and neighborhoods. After integration, the Black woman was favored over the Black man. Hiring a Black woman made it possible to fill two minority positions at once: she was both African American as well as female. The Black woman became more acceptable to society than the Black man. This divisive maneuver took its toll on the Black family, the Black male in particular, and drove many men away. No longer was the Black man, in many cases the major financial contributor to the family unit.

The 1980's ushered in an era of increased single-family homes that were run by women who needed strength. What better source of strength than the church? The church was a source of community and strength as well as spiritual growth (Williamson, 2010). Consider these scriptures from the Word of God:

> The Lord [is] my strength and my shield; my heart trusted in him, and I am helped: therefore, my heart greatly rejoiceth; and with my song will I praise him (Psalm 28:7)

> I will lift up mine eyes unto the hills, from whence cometh my help (Psalm 121:1)
>
> My help [cometh] from the LORD, which made heaven and earth (Psalm 121:2)
>
> The Lord [is] my rock, and my fortress, and my deliverer; my God, my God, my strength, in whom I will trust; my buckler, and the horn of my salvation, [and] my high tower (Psalm 18:2)

An enormous amount of research has been done focusing on the reasons that men's attendance, in every denomination and in every age group, does not equal the church attendance of women. While the number of Black men incarcerated and killed in "Black on Black" crime incidents continues to top the Bureau of Justice charts each year, the number of Black men in African-American churches continues to drop. Many believe there is a domino effect at hand: the Black church is failing Black men, black men are failing the Black community, and the black community is failing the black family (Akinyemi, 2008). We have a Male Crisis (lack of males) in the church as well as a Men Crisis (lack of males developing into quality and productive men). Whatever the reasons, we need to find ways to minister to these men. We need them now!

In his work, Toler (1995) has concluded that the most effective way to reduce Black crime, and to strengthen Black families, may be to return African American men to their spiritual roots. Malidome Some has suggested that men of faith need to be in pockets of prayer groups and men's study groups to encourage each other's quest to be better husbands, fathers, and leaders.

Males who attend church regularly tend to fall into three age groups: 1) birth to early teens, 2) twenty-somethings to fifty-somethings, and 3) older men who establish church membership when their health begins to fail. Of the young boys who attend church over 70 % of them will abandon it during their teens and twenties. Many of these boys will never return. The few adult men in the second group are usually active not only in black churches but in the community as well. Many times, this leads them to make tough choices with where to spend their limited amount of spare time.

Pastor Fredrick Robinson, of Mount Gilead Missionary Baptist Church in Atlanta said: "You've heard the saying that the Black man is in jail waiting for justice and Black woman is in church waiting for Jesus." Young Black males are looking for African-American men who are "man enough to tell us what to do." Young black females raised by their mothers are longing for positive father figures, also. "How can a 16-year-old girl choose the right man if she has never seen one?"

"Five groups", Kunjufu said, "generally have the greatest problem believing in Christianity and Jesus: those who are male, those who are educated, those who are young, those who are Afrocentric, and those who are wealthy. And don't let a brother have all five."

Research reveals that church growth is greatest among congregations with healthy male participation. Jesus had no trouble getting men to follow him. They readily cast down their nets, stopped collecting taxes, and left their families in order to become fishers of men. It is difficult to convince some men today to get out of bed and/or drop their remote controls for a few hours a week to join others in serving the Lord.

CHAPTER VI

WHY BLACK MEN DON'T ATTEND CHURCH?

Pulpit Pimps

Black men are deterred from coming to church because of the perceived and actual occupation of Pulpit Pimps. Pulpit Pimps are no different than a pimp on the street, they just use their God given talent in the pulpit to earn money. They pimp the congregation by brainwashing them into believing anything to get what they want (Quezada, 2010). Today's pulpit pimps, side with their worldly colleagues by:

1. Dressing the same i.e., custom made suits that cost thousands of dollars, alligator and ostrich shoes that go for $1500 per pair, stylish jewelry and eye-wear).
2. Riding around in the same cars such as Bentleys, Lexus and Rolls Royce Phantoms parked in the pastors parking spot. They fly in G4 corporate jets to preach the word because flying commercial airlines isn't expedient enough for them.
3. Residing in affluent mansions located in gated communities to keep them away from ordinary people.

Everyone familiar with the "Pimping Game" knows that in order to become a skillful pimp the pimp has to gain the confidence of his prostitutes (deceived Christians who give offerings with mistaken motivations). The deceived and not fully matured believer thinks that this "consecrated pimp" is the foundation of blessings and only through the pimp/preacher is he or she safe from harm. In other words, only through the anointing of this pimping reverend can the blessings of God flow. (Johnson, 2012). They will frequently give you a point of contact such as handkerchiefs, miracle oil, unusual anointed spring water or some small ornament, even merely placing your hands on the television. Covetousness will always be one of the uniqueness of the Pimping Preacher.

In response to the survey question "What are your thoughts about the pastor", this question was in the top tier of negativity and elicited a substantial amount of negative answers compared to other questions in the survey. Seventy percent (70%) of the participants pictured preachers as pulpit pimps; they also connected them to a love of money. These pimping preachers make use of false doctrine to coerce the flock to give more money for their personal ministry (Johnson, n. d., p. 1). "They only want money" (all respondents but 5 and 10) or "They only want money…con artists." (Respondent 8). Some televangelists have generated negative attention to the ministry by their love for bling; multimillion dollar estates, luxury cars, vacation homes, outlandish trips and private jets (Pinsky, 2008). Close review of the respondents' statements led the researcher to conclude that the negative media attention has left the participants with the perception that all pastors are comparable to preachers who preach a prosperity gospel. Respondent 6 reiterated the sentiments of most the participants: "These pastors just want money and too many of them preach a prosperity gospel; I hate that. They hustle the people". Respondent 8 reported: "The pastors are con-artists, want money. An example is Creflo Dollar who asked people to buy him a new jet when he already had a jet; the sad thing is they bought the jet for him. There is no confidence in him being a man of God".

The television show "Preachers of L.A." gives a bad impression of preachers. During the 1960s, prosperity preachers embraced televangelism that was pioneered by Oral Roberts who traded his tent revivals for a television program that became the most watched religious show in America (Robins, 2010). Reverend Ike, an African American pastor from New York City, set in motion the prosperity philosophy in the late 1960s. He soon had extensive television programs and became distinguished for his ostentatious style and smooth talk. His candidness about love for material possessions and teachings about the "Science of the Mind" led many evangelists to shun him (Harrell, 1975). In the 1980s, prosperity teachings became very popular in the United States because of the influence of well-known televangelists such as Jim Bakker. Bakker's influence faded after he was accused in a high-profile scandal, subsequently he was tried and sent to prison (Smith, 2010). The after effects of Bakker's fall opened the door for Trinity Broadcasting Network (TBN) to emerge as the overriding force in prosperity televangelism, having brought Robert Tilton and Benny Hinn to notoriety (Robins, 2010).

The Neo-Pentecostal movement gained greater acceptance within charismatic Christianity during the late 1990s as they embraced prosperity teachings (Coleman, 2000). Three of the four largest congregations in the United States were teaching prosperity theology by 2006, and Joel Osteen has been recognized for spreading it outside of the Pentecostal and Charismatic movement through his books (Smith, 2010). Bruce Wilkinson's The Prayer of Jabez sold millions of copies and encouraged readers to seek prosperity (Jenkins, 2006). A 2006 poll by Time conveyed that 17 percent of Christians in America said they associated with the movement (Van Biema, 2008). There is no sanctioned governing body for the movement, though many ministries are informally interrelated (Coleman, 2000).

Money focused churches led by prosperity driven pastors tend to be run on unusual schemes. One of these unusual arrangements is the division of the church into exclusive circles: the all-powerful pastor settled at the center, the inner-circle of conformist around him consisting of the pastor's understudies and the church's rich and/or famous, and the outer- circle of the everyday people who aspire to be in the inner-circle. The power of those in the inner-circle is governed by the amount of favor the pastor confers upon them. To gain more esteem the inner-circle will employ many favor-enhancing measures, one of which is an arrangement called honoring the pastor. It works like this, the inner-circle determine what the pastor would like to have for his birthday. Then the inner-circle will pressure the outer-circle for the funds to buy the gifts. Pastors have been given diamond rings, large amounts of cash, all expenses paid cruises, cars, boats, and innumerable other expensive items. The pastors are complicit in this scheme. Rather than ask for the gifts outright, they have others do the work for them. They could discourage such action by refusing the gifts when they are presented and instruct the people to use God's money more wisely by giving to a nobler cause, but they never do (Cultwatch, n. d). One respondent in this study believed the modern-day prosperity preachers accumulated their wealth by hustling the poor, "They only want money… hustlers". (Respondent 6). Some prosperity churches have a reputation for maneuvering and defrauding the poor (Clifton, 2009).

In Barna's (2017) "The State of Pastors" report, generated in collaboration with Pepperdine University, the acceptance of pastors was generally apathetic. According to the report, 1 in 5 adults in the United States feel that pastors are not effective or sincere. Only 24 percent of U.S. adults maintain a "very positive" option of pastors in general. Nineteen percent hold a "negative" opinion, and nine percent profess a "very negative" opinion.

They have to work

Depending on which survey you read, the average American is spending between 47 and 49 hours a week at work. Of those varying figures, they all agree that Americans work more hours every year. Edelen (2004) in his book *The Churches Missing Men* observed that as companies further downsize and ask more of their workers, this trend seems to be without end. With the constant threat of downsizing and layoffs men feel the need to work as much as they can in order to provide a level of financial security for their families. Sacrificing their own spiritual growth seems to be a small price to pay for keeping their families out of the clutches of the debt collectors.

Too Many Collections

With rising unemployment, higher taxes, and other financial woes, the last thing any man wants to see when he goes to church is a pastor with his hand out asking for more than his fair share of a brother's income. Paul Johnson, a mailroom supervisor, was totally disgusted when he said, "before I could put my wallet away from the first offering, a battalion of collection plates would bombard me again. At one point, I thought I'd have to start paying admission."

Services are Too Long

While the collections are too numerous for some, prosperity teachings offend others, the lengthy services turn some African American men away from church. Depending on the denomination, on any given Sunday there could be up to five different collections, two or more choirs, each singing two to three songs, announcements, and pastor's comments, as well as an obligatory forty-five minutes (minimum) sermon. Don't forget the altar call and prayers.

Father Did Not Attend Church

In response to the question "How often did your father attend church?" the majority (60%) of the respondents said they "don't know" if their father attended church. This was an indication that the father was not living in the home (Thomas, Krampe and Newton, 2007; U.S. Census Bureau, 2017), not married to the mother (Lee, 2017) or the contact with the father was null or sporadic, as indicated by respondent 1 who stated, "I don't know, we didn't have a relationship". The United States Census data from 2010 brought to light that more African American families comprised of single parent mothers than married homes with both parents (Lofquist, et al, 2010). Most recently, it was communicated that 72% of Black babies were born to unwed mothers (Riley, 2012; Washington, 2010). Glick's study found that single parent homes are twice as prevailing in African American families as they are in other racial groups, and this difference continues to broaden (1997). Perhaps statistics like these evoked responses like "I am not very close to my father ..." (Respondent 3); "I never knew my father that well," (Respondent 5); "I barely knew him, I don't know how often he went to church," (Respondent 6); "My father was never around and I had no relationship with him," (Respondent 7) and "I don't know, I didn't know my dad that well." (Respondent 9).

Data from the United States Census reports made known that between 1880 and 1960, married households comprising two parent homes were the most prevalent form of African American family structures; then in 1960 single parent homes rose dramatically (Akerlof, Yellen, and Katz, 1996; Ruggles, 1994). One reason for the depressed rates of African American marriages since 1960 is elevated age of first marriage for numerous African Americans. The marriage rate increases with age for African American women compared to white Americans who follow the same tendencies but marry at younger ages than African Americans (Dixon, 2009). Fewer employment opportunities and a weakening in real earnings for Black males since 1960 are also identified as sources of increasing marital unpredictability (Ruggles, 1997). One form of marriage that has waned is the shotgun marriage (Akerlof, Yellen, and Katz, 1996). A shotgun wedding is a wedding that is arranged to circumvent embarrassment due to premarital sex conceivably leading to an unplanned pregnancy, rather than out of the desire of the couple (Dictionary.com, 2016). Also, before the 1970s, the custom was such that, should a couple have a pregnancy out of wedlock, marriage was expected (Akerlof, Yellen, and Katz, 1996). Social norms have subsequently changed, giving women and men the option to decide if, and when they should get married (Akerlof, Yellen, and Katz, 1996).

In general, fathers living with their children participated in their children's lives to a greater degree than fathers who live apart from their children (Jones and Mosher, 2013A Boston University study by Coley and Medeiros (2007) noted that Black fathers who don't reside in the home are more likely to maintain consistent contact with their children than fathers of any other ethnic group. Some 37% of white biological fathers have had at least one child out of wedlock, while 77% have had a birth inside a marriage. Among African American men, 72% have had a child out of wedlock, and 48% have had one within marriage (Livingston and Parker, 2011). Pew Research Center (2011) also conveyed that Black biological fathers are far less likely than white biological fathers to be married to the mother of their children; some 36% of Black fathers are married to their child's mother, compared with 59% of white fathers. While about 21% of white fathers live separately from at least one of their children, this number rises to 35% among Hispanic fathers, and 44% among African American fathers (Livingston and Parker, 2011).

In this situation, African American single mothers see themselves performing the role of the mother and the father (Burgess and Brown, 2000; Wilson, 2017). According to Burgess and Brown, the single mother's responsibility is greater than a married mother since she does not have a husband to provide a second party income for her family members. This lack of a second party income has resulted in the majority of African American children raised in single mother households having inadequate rearing (2000).

Some men do not have a close relationship with their father due to high incarceration rates of African American men. "I am not very close to my father, he was incarcerated a lot ..." (Respondent 3). As of 2014 approximately 12–13% of the American population is African American, but they make up 35% of jail inmates, and 37% of prison inmates of the 2.2 million male inmates (Alexander, 2010; Minton and Zeng, 2015). According to Hattery and Smith (2007), 25–33% of African-American men are spending time in jail or prison. The majority of Black men are incarcerated for illicit drug related charges, primarily marijuana. The irony is that studies show that African American male illegal drug use and sale rates are similar to other racial and ethnic groups (Alexander, 2010; Minton and Zeng, 2015). According to Johnston, et al (2007) African Americans had substantially lower rates of use of licit and illicit drugs than do whites. Incarceration prolongs poverty, single parenthood, and the separation of family units.

A study performed by Vaidyanathan (2011), found an unrelenting direct parental impact on offspring's future religiosity. Research executed by Bader and Desmond (2006) suggested the more religious behaviors parents exhibit i.e. church attendance and the more affirmative their attitudes towards religion for example, the value they place on religion the more immense the transfer of religiosity to their children. For all outcome measures, children of unswervingly religious parents displayed higher levels of religiosity than children reared by parents lacking religious consistency. If Dad takes faith in God seriously then the message to their children is that God should be taken seriously (Craven, 2011). "He attended church at least 3 times a week." Respondent 4. The father of respondent 4 was a minister which helped to explain his frequent attendance. Merrill and colleagues (2001) suggested that indifference among parents may be instilled in their children, thus hindering the protective factor of religiosity as was reported by respondent 2, "My father never attended church when I was growing up. My parents divorced when I was very young. He remarried when I was 12 years old." Respondent 10 revealed, "My daddy never sat his feet in the church, he did not go in the church at his own mother's funeral; he stood outside." Respondent 8 reported that his father attended church: "Very seldom, 5 times a year."

Thus, most men in this study lacked paternal influence to attend church through father absence. Perhaps the reason why some fathers are not involved with their children is because they are not religious. Religious fathers are more involved fathers. This finding holds for both married and divorced men (King, 2003). The majority (60%) lacked a meaningful, consistent relationship with their father which is contrary to a study by Coley who noted that Black fathers who don't reside in the home are more likely to maintain consistent contact with their children than fathers of any other ethnic group (2007). Thus, out of all the influences for positive outcomes including religiosity in the lives of young Black men, the one that is most important is missing. African American boys need a positive father figure.

The importance of the father in the home cannot be over emphasized; he (the father) is the single most important figure in the family when it comes to religiosity and influencing the family to engage in public worship. If the mother is the first to accept Christ and becomes a Christian, there is a 17 % probability everyone else in the household will follow. But if the father is first, there is a 93 % possibility everyone else in the household will follow (House, 2003). Jesus revealed how to grow a vigorous church; focus on men first. Christ loved everyone including women and children, but he spent most of his time and energy cultivating and instructing a handful of men. He knew a truth many churches have forgotten; if you convert men, you transform the family, the community and the society. Attract a man to church, and you frequently get the family in the bargain.

Being reared by a non-religious father is correlated with increased problematic behavior among young offspring. Petts study suggested that religious communities may be a resource that encourages fathers to be more involved in their family life and encourage positive development among children (Petts, 2009a). Churches and the leadership should focus on attracting and reaching out to men; by so doing the churches will be healthy and vibrant. Morley (2008) suggested that there are three prerequisites to reaching unchurched men. The prerequisites are: (1) The senior pastor must be an enthusiastic supporter of men's ministry, (2) The senior pastor, an associate pastor, or a lay leader who is passionate about reaching men must be designated as the leader and (3) The right strategy is imperative to making things work. The church men's ministry program must decide to win lost men, to call Christian men to a deeper commitment, to make disciples of these men, and to equip and call these men to personal ministry (p. 2).

Mother Did Not Attend Church

It is difficult to determine which parent had more influence on their sons' church attendance since most of the respondents were unaware of their fathers' religiosity; sixty percent (60%) of the respondents said they "don't know" if their father attended church. Dickie, et al (2006) observed that it is the religious socialization of children by their mothers that suggests that mothers are the primary influence on the development of young adults' concept of God. Even in adulthood, parents, especially mothers, continue to exercise influence on their sons' and daughters' religious sensitivities and concepts of God. In the case of nurturance, parents influence how their children feel about themselves, which in turn shapes concepts of God as loving, warm, and nurturing. The influence of the mother is questionable since thirty percent (30%) of the mothers attended church at least once per week as related by respondents 1, 7 and 10; respondent 5 reported that his mother attended church twice per week. This meant that at least forty percent (40%) of the mothers were regular church attenders. Reinert, and Edwards (2012) tested Hertel and Donahue's (1995) hypothesis, for which they found some support according to Social Learning Theory, children form images of God primarily through the influence of the same sex parent as part of the sex role socialization process. Thus, mothers' influence will be greater on daughters than on sons and fathers' influence will be greater on sons than on daughters (Hertel and Donahue, 1995). Research performed by Reinert and Edwards (2012); Hertel and Donahue (1995), indicated that the mother's influence was ineffectual as it relates to the current study; 60% of the respondents were unaware of the father's church attendance which means they were stuck with the only religious influence they knew and that was the mother. In the more intimate dimensions of religiosity, namely attachment to God and the view of God as a loving God, the level of attachment security to the same sex parent is more influential than attachment to the opposite sex parent in both males and females (Reinert and Edwards, 2012). Reinert and Edwards findings do not concur with House (2003) who stated that the father has more influence on the entire family than the mother when it comes to religiosity. Carothers (2005) posited that children with more religious mothers had fewer internalizing and externalizing difficulties at age ten (10) than those who did not have religious mothers.

A Dutch study was performed where data were collected where 474 participants were questioned in 1983 as adolescences and in 2007 as adults. In 2007 the respondents on reflection answered questions about how they were reared by their parents. Analysis revealed that juvenile church attendance depended primarily on parental and more particularly on maternal church attendance, whereas adult church attendance is essentially a consequence of juvenile church attendance (Vermeer, Janssen and Scheepers, 2012). Thus, young people whose mothers went to church were more likely to become churchgoers themselves, whereas those who went to church as youngsters were more likely to continue going to church as adults. Respondents 3 and 9 reported that their mother attended church four times a year; respondents 6 and 8 communicated that their mother attended church five times per year. Respondent 2 recounted that his mother never attended church.

Even when both parents are present in the home, most researchers recognized the father for having more influence in the sphere of religiosity. Numerous studies have minimized the influence of the mother and emphasized the father's impact on their children's church attendance. In Switzerland, the Fertility and Family Survey was commissioned by the Federal Statistical Office (Switzerland) to enable Switzerland to take part in an international project initiated by the UNECE Population Activities Unit. The survey was conducted by the Council of Europe between October 1994 and May 1995, with the findings being published in 2000 by the Council of Europe. The results were representative of Switzerland's perpetual resident population aged 20–49 (Haug and Wanner, 2000). The findings revealed that if a father does not go to church, no matter how faithful his wife's religious fervor, only one child in 50 will become a regular participant. If a father does go regularly, irrespective of the practice of the mother, between two-thirds and three-quarters of their children will become churchgoers (regular and irregular). If a father goes but erratically to church, regardless of his wife's devoutness, between half and two-thirds of their offspring will attend church frequently or irregularly. A non-practicing mother with a consistent father will see at least two-thirds of her children ending up at church. In contrast, a non-practicing father with a regular mother will witness two-thirds of his children not attending church. If his wife is similarly intermittent that figure rises to 80 percent (Low, 2003).

A study by Bruce and Bruce, (1996) found comparable results on the influence of fathers: When both parents attend Sunday school, 72% of the children attend Sunday school when they reach adulthood. When only the father attends Sunday school, 55% of the children attend when grown. When only the mother attends Sunday school, 15% of the children attend when they are full-grown adult. When neither parent attends Sunday school, only 6% of the children attend when grown. A survey by Horner, Ralston and Sunde (1996) found fathers to be highly influential in the matter of religiosity including church attendance. If a child is the first person in a household to become a Christian, there is a 3.5% probability everyone else in the household will follow. If the mother is the first to become a Christian, there is a 17% probability everyone else in the household will follow. However, when the father is first, there is a 93% probability everyone else in the household will follow (Horner, Ralston and Sunde, 1996). Fathers hold the key to the salvation of the family, specifically the children. Winning and keeping men is crucial to the community of faith and fundamental to the work of all mothers and the future redemption of our children (Low, 2003).

They Have Lost Faith in God

Unfortunately, many men have lost their faith in God. Where there is no faith there is no desire to set foot inside a house of worship. Pastor Clarence James, lecturer and author of a series chronicling African American history and culture said, "Given the state of America, I can empathize with the men who refuse to believe that God would allow this country to become such a rancid place. But things can only get worse if our men stop believing and lose faith."

Listed below are some alarming facts to reflect on:

- 83% of people arrested for serious crimes are men;
- A man is 2500% more likely to end up in a state prison than a woman;
- 87% of drunk drivers are men

- Men are more apt to die from cancer, strokes, and heart attacks than women;
- Men are the ones who die in 75% of all suicides;
- Men commit 85% of all murders in America.

The Church is Hypocritical

Immoral behavior such as embezzlement and stealing by ministers and church leaders were cited as reasons why men avoid the church. Yes, some of that has occurred in churches, but our commitment should be to Christ, and not to any man or person that makes up the church. A survey of U.S. adults, who don't go to church, even on the holidays, finds that 72% believe that God, or a supreme being exists. 72% believe the church is full of hypocrites. "Indeed, 44% agree with the statement "Christians get on my nerves" (Grossman, 2008).

Lack of Tact in the Pulpit

Several men interviewed in a survey verbalized that the church is unsympathetic to their plights. Why, they reason, should they go to church to listen to the pastor attack them in his sermon? By not attending church, men feel powerful and in control because they are finally able to challenge authority and get away with it. The church needs to be more sensitive to the fact that a man wants to hear that he is doing a good job.

You Can't Preach

> "Contrary to popular opinion, bad preaching isn't when the preacher reads his sermon, mumbles or bores his audience. That is merely bad delivery. No, bad preaching is preaching that does not rightly proclaim God's Word of Law and God's Word of Gospel to sinners" (Walther, 2010).

Many preachers make their congregations suffer through their lack of quality delivery. The message may be scripturally sound, but no one hears it. It has been said that good preaching won't necessarily fill a church, but research is clear that poor preaching will empty it. As Christianity Today reports, "Researchers found that 82 percent of Protestants and 76 percent of all regular worshipers consider sermons' biblical lessons as a major factor that draws them to services." They also desire relevance: "80 percent of Protestants and 75 percent of worshipers valued sermons that connect faith to everyday life" (Stonestreet and Guthrie, 2017). Rick Warren has said that some pastors can take the most exciting book in the world and bore people to tears. "The tragedy of being a boring speaker is that it causes people to think God is boring!"

Church is Just Church

The importance of attending church is lost on many men. They believe that the myriad of other things they have to do and places they have to go supersedes church activities. When everything else is done that they want to do, or perhaps when they retire then they will have the time for church.

> "We have the same problem that Jesus had, but he was not afraid to attack the Scribes and Pharisees who were in control of the community because He knew they were being used by the enemy....our churches also are being used to destroy our unity. Our churches are being used to block both political and economic unity. Our churches are being used against us.... You can't free a people as long as their leaders are taking orders from the enemy " (Cleage, 1995).

The Church is Not Relevant to the Community

The question was asked, "How relevant do you think the Black church is to the Black community?" This part of the research showed that the vast majority of the participants perceived the Black church as an irrelevant establishment in the community. Sewell (2001) doubts that Black faith communities are concerned about the advancement of their neighborhoods. Chavest and Higginst (1992) suggest that the Black church may care but the centrality of the Black church within African American communities has been compromised, by added competition from secular organizations more suitable to meet the needs of differentiated inner-city communities, and by improved opportunities for African Americans in secular, social, political, and economic domains. Davis (2013) believes there is a crisis in Black America and the Black church refuses or is unable to address the crisis because the church is in a state of unconsciousness. Davis also maintains that the irrelevant church rejects the notion to take the necessary steps to diminish oppression and eventually eliminate it. It puts resources in non-liberating activities which adds to conditions of deficit already experienced by the poor and oppressed. A total of ninety percent (90%) of the respondents in this study described the church as an unconnected element in the community. Statements such as "Not relevant at all, they do no help the Black community" (Respondent 1) were commonplace. A respondent communicated "They don't give back to the community. The church takes in money but they don't do anything to help people." (Respondent 3). The accepted perception of the Black church has been inclined to focus on the inward, "other-world," perspective (Pinkney, 1993). The Black church is liable for its general lack of concern for the ethical, moral, social and collective well-being of the community. It has been accommodating (Essien-Udom, 1962), choosing to focus its attention solely on eternal life rather than focus on the problems confronting people in their everyday lives (Wingfield, 1988). Moreover, this kind of reaction from the church elicited statements like "Not relevant at all … they don't help the community at all, they exist only for themselves." (Respondent 6). "They are not spiritual, it is run like a business and they watch the bottom line. There is no outreach. They don't care." (Respondent 4); "It's all about them." (Respondent 9); "The church is not relevant at all. It is not about reaching out for souls." (Respondent 10). The Black church has been somewhat ineffective and insignificant

(Myrdal, 1971). One respondent (Respondent 7) pointed to the fact that there is not a lack of money or resources in the Black community: "The Black church brings in around over a billion dollars a week. They don't build schools, hospitals, etc. The churches need to take some of their money and invest in the community." The billion dollars a week figure is somewhat overstated considering that Black churches, in aggregate, have collected only a little more than $420nbillion in tithes and donations from 1980 to 2013 (Furious, 2013). The overall consumerism of Black America is enough to run a third world country; yet, Blacks in America do not produce, control, or distribute the goods and services needed in the African American Community (Brown, 2005 cited in Davis, 2013). The Black church is the primary institution that can empower the Black community. To empower is to help people get in touch with the power that is theirs (Ali, 1999). Perhaps this was what respondent 7 meant when he said, "The churches need to take some of their money and invest in the community." The other-worldliness of the Black church dismisses the hardships, adversities, suffering and inequalities of this world as transitory and short-lived (Frazier, 1964).

There were other scholarly perspectives on the subject and some of them described the Black church as positive, progressive and relevant. Over the years, an incontestable and plausible body of evidence has emphasized the importance of African American churches as conduits for political skills, resources, and mobilization (Assensoh and Assensoh, 2001; Barnes, 2005; Butler, Booth, and Burwell, 2012; Carlton-LaNey, 2006). The contributions the Black church has made to the community may have gone unnoticed as indicated by this respondent's statement: "It is relevant but what is being done is not being noticed by the community." (Respondent 8). Gallop (2001), showed that African Americans give the church high ratings for the ability to solve community problems. They also viewed their churches as having the best chance of alleviating social problems that afflict their communities compared to any other institution.

To be viewed by most African Americans as a relevant organization again, the church needs to be more active in matters that impact the lives of Black people. If Black Christians really want to show that they are relevant, they must tackle the systemic issues of poverty that force Black parents to buy and feed their children sweetened and unhealthy foods that lead to diabetes and heart disease but cost so much less than fresh fruits and vegetables. The church needs to emphasize the whole person including the scriptural instruction that says, "The body is the temple of God" (1 Corinthians 6:19), and it is the will of God that the body be kept healthy. The Black church must emulate ministers who led the civil rights movement and tackle the issues of racism and broken families that lead young Black men to believe they have no way to get ahead except by adopting a life of crime. The Black church needs to learn how to articulate a message and create a movement that will hold the police accountable for the execution of Black men and boys. We live in a culture that wants quick and simple solutions that require nominal effort; but these will not be simple fixes.

During the civil rights movement of the 1960s the Black church was the voice against social inequity, discrimination and unfairness and organized and financed protests (Fitzgerald and Spohn, 2005; Lincoln and Mamiya, 1990). Today the Black church is conveniently silent during the Black Lives Matter protests; it appears that the church is behaving like spectators at a sporting event. There is a heavy weight of being Black in a world that detests Black existence (Pierce, 2015). The Black church must become active in the community again and start lifting some of the weight that plague Black people. The question the church must ask itself: Is the theology we espouse expansive enough to address the world in which we live, or are we one year, 10 years, or even 50 years behind the times? The Black church must teach young people the value of civic involvement by including them in the process and actions (Smetana and Metzger, 2005). Our commitment within our churches to declare unequivocally and categorically, that "Black lives matter," is just one essential step in healing the wounds of a grieving people (Pierce, 2015). Jamal Bryant, pastor and founder of Empowerment Temple AME Church in Baltimore, Maryland, said Black Lives Matter is the first civil rights movement in America that isn't being led by the Church and clergy are not on the frontlines (Blair, 2016). Bryant challenged clergy to take off their robes and hit the street corner and do something that will change where it is that we are going. The church cannot presume that America is a colorblind society; it is not and never has been. The civil rights movement in the 1960s concentrated on the civil and political rights that were disallowed to Black people—access and use of public accommodations, the right to vote, and guaranteeing fair employment and housing opportunities—it did not directly confront the racialized humiliation Black people sustained, and many continue to endure, at the hands of the police. What the Black Lives Matter protests have done, however, is not only put police reform on the policy agenda but demanded that American society reconsider how it values Black lives (Harris, 2015). Black lives should matter to policemen who pledge to serve and protect yet murder Black children as if they are insignificant. It appears that Black life does not matter, therefore the Black church must live up to its mission to value all life and demand that human beings regardless of race, creed or color be treated with dignity and respect.

Davis (2010) believes the black church has to stand with the poor and oppressed as Jesus did, and fight the injustices of our day. If the church does not become an active part of the solution, then they have become a part of the problem. Today you will find that churches by the thousands are protesting homosexuality, and/or abortions. The passion with which many speak is very real. However, where is the compassion for little black children who are living in poverty? What about using some of that enthusiasm to apply pressure to those who have the power to create jobs or health care reform? " Bishop Charles E. Blake Sr., the Presiding Bishop of the Church of God in Christ, appears to be a solitary voice in the wilderness when he announced COGIC's support of healthcare reform with the public option" (Glaude, 2010).

CHAPTER VII

CHURCH IS GOOD FOR MEN AND MEN ARE GOOD FOR CHURCH

Churchgoers are more likely to be married and express a higher level of satisfaction with life. Church involvement is the most important predictor of marital stability and happiness (The Heritage Foundation, 1996). Church involvement moves people out of poverty. It's also correlated with less depression, more self esteem and greater family and marital happiness.

The Pew Research Center (2006) found that people who attend religious services weekly or more are happier (43% very happy) than those who attend monthly or less (31%); or seldom or never (26%). This relationship between happiness and incidence of church attendance has been a steady finding in the General Social Surveys taken over the years.

A similar pattern applies within all main religious denominations. For instance, 38% of all Catholics who attend church weekly or more report being very happy, while just 28% of Catholics who attend church less often say they are very happy. The survey also finds that white evangelical Protestants (43%) are more likely than white mainline Protestants (33%) to report being very happy, but this difference goes away after taking frequency of church attendance into account.

Religious participation leads men to become more engaged husbands and fathers. Teens with religious fathers are more likely to say they enjoy spending time with dad and that they admire him (Smith and Kim, 1997). Fathers who attend services several times a month or more are 95% more likely to be married when their child is born, whereas mothers who attend regularly are 40% more likely to be married at this time. If both attend their odds of marriage to one another are even higher.

Religious attendance is associated with a 67% increase in the odds of marriage for an unmarried mother if the father is a regular churchgoer and a 55% increase if the mother is a regular churchgoer. Their odds of marriage are even higher if they both attend religious services several times a month or more (Wilcox, 2007).

Being involved in a church consistently decreases levels of deviant behavior and crime. Religious involvement decreases domestic violence among both men and women according to a national study (Ellison and Anderson, 2001). Church attendance has also been associated with decreased levels of assault, burglary, and larceny (Bainbridge, 1989), and religiosity promotes decreased levels of violent crime (Hummer, et al, 1999; Lester, 1987).

The Barna report (2011) indicates that the sector that possesses viewpoints most likely to align with those taught in the Bible during the past 20 years are blacks. On five of the eight faith factors, blacks were more likely than either whites or Hispanics to mirror a scriptural view. Particularly, blacks were more likely than other groups to say:

- Their religious beliefs are very significant in their life today
- They have made a personal dedication to Jesus Christ that is still important in their life today
- They believe that God is "the all-knowing, all-powerful and faultless Creator of the universe who still rules the world today"
- They vigorously agree that the Bible is totally correct in all of the principles it teaches
- They have a conscientiousness to share their religious beliefs with other people who might believe differently than they do.

The Barna Group also examined religious behaviors and discovered that blacks stood out on five of the six behaviors. Specifically, the study shows that blacks were the most likely to:

- Engage in church activities, such as attending church services, attending a Sunday school class, and volunteering at their church during the week
- Read the Bible, other than at church during a typical week
- Blacks were the least likely segment to be unchurched. In fact, they were only half as likely as either whites or Hispanics to be unchurched.

Greater Longevity

Insurance studies show regular church attendance adds 5.7 years to your life. In a Duke University study of 2391 people who were at least 65 years old found that regular churchgoers who also prayed daily or studied the Bible daily were 40 % less likely to have high blood pressure than those who did not. Elderly churchgoers had better mental health and were less likely to have high degrees of a protein associated with age-related illness.

Greater longevity is constantly and significantly related to higher levels of religious participation and involvement, regardless of the sex, race, education, or health history of those studied (Johnson, et al, "Objective Hope"). Those who are religiously involved live an average of seven years longer than those who are not. This gap is as great as that between non-smokers and those who smoke a pack of cigarettes a day. Predicting the life spans of 20-year-olds who are religiously involved compared with those who are not yields differences in life span as great as those between women and men and between whites and blacks (Regnerus, 2003). Among African Americans, the longevity benefit is still greater. The average life span of religious blacks is 14 years longer than that of their nonreligious peers (Hummer, Rogers, Nam and Ellison, 1999). Furthermore, religious service attendance appears to contribute to quality of life and good health for substantial proportions of elderly people (Levin, 1994; McFadden, 1996; Neill and Kahn, 1999). Attendance at church may improve the health status of urban African Americans by increasing the likelihood of preventive health practices (Aaron, Levine and Burstin, 2003).

Attending church services on a regular basis can not only improve the quantity of your life, but the quality as well. In 3 John: 2 we find that God wants us "to prosper and be in health, even as thy soul prospereth." We are reminded in Deuteronomy 8:18 that it is by God's grace that he gives us the power to get wealth.

There is a special peace of mind that only God can give. "Peace I give to you; not as the world give do I give to you. Let not your heart be troubled, neither let it be afraid" (John 14:27)

God will give you courage and strength. "Be strong and of good courage, do not fear nor be afraid of them; for the Lord your God, He is the One who goes with you. He will not leave you nor forsake you" (Deuteronomy 31: 6)

Happiness and Well-Being

Happy people tend to be industrious and law-abiding and also tend to learn well, thus having an affirmative impact on humanity. Religion significantly affects the level of an individual's happiness and overall sense of security. In the vast majority of the studies reviewed, an increase in religious practice was coupled with having greater hope and a greater sense of purpose in life (Johnson et al, "Objective Hope"). Religious participation and activities are positive resources for many adults in solving problems and dealing with difficult life issues (Barusch, 1999; Cutler and Hendricks, 2000).

Learning to love others the way God loves you is a source of happiness and comfort. Learning to forgive yourself and others can literally heal your body and your soul.

Coping Skills

Church membership can enhance coping skills. One study found that people were much more apt to use positive coping responses when they received spiritual support from fellow church members (Krause, et al, 2001).

Men are good for church

A study from Hartford Seminary found that in order to promote church growth, health, and harmony men must be involved in the church (Hadaway, 2005). It has been observed by some that men have the greatest influence on the family's church attendance. He says "…if a child gets saved, 4 % of the family will follow. If a mother gets saved, 17 % of the family will follow, but if a man gets saved, 93 % of the family will follow." Saving a man, it appears, would mean saving the whole family, too (WhyChurch.org.uk, 2011).

In the African-American family it has been found that boys who live with two parents, especially their own married parents, enjoy greater economic security and better parenting. Furthermore, when black fathers are present in the home, they are able to provide a real-life example of what it means to be a black man (Malone-Colon and Roberts, 2006). These fathers are in a better position to teach their sons the attitudes and skills needed to negotiate the challenges of being a black man in America.

Of course, many African American single mothers do an exceptional job of successfully raising their children. However, scholars have noted that some African American mothers sometimes expect and require less of their sons than they do their daughters. Girls are expected to get good grades in school in addition to their responsibilities at home. Boys are seldom assigned household chores. In essence, some mothers seem to "raise their daughters, and love their sons." "Who is going to teach black boys to be responsible for their education, employment, and overall skill development?" (Kunjufu, 1997).

Boys are more affected than girls are by their fathers' absence. There is no masculine role model for them. Girls, on the other hand, do have a prominent role model of femininity that does not depend on the presence of a father (Beaty, 1995). Boys have other men as role models, but they are usually not as close or important as a parent would be (Hofferth and Anderson, 2003). Fathers are more likely to stress masculine traits in their sons and feminine traits in their daughters.

Dr. Marian Wright (May 2010) suggests we are facing a new kind of slavery. It has been called the "cradle to prison pipeline." If we don't do something about this, and soon, we will lose even more of our men making the social and racial progress of the last 50 years null and void. Black churches have to become the force behind the movement to save our children. "As of 2004, more African American men were disenfranchised due to felony disenfranchisement laws than in 1870, the year that the 15th Amendment was ratified prohibiting laws that explicitly deny the right to vote on the basis of race." Dr. Wright continues with the fact that in "1980 only 100,000 black men were incarcerated…In 2010 there [were] 1.5 million black males in prison and the major reason [was] crack cocaine."

African American men are challenged in this twenty-first century to redefine what it means to be a man and to redefine masculinity. The definition of a strong black man is in need of retooling. Far too many black men accept the European model of man as the unquestionable ruler of the household. The wife suffers unrealistic self oppression in this scenario. "If we as men are expected to be stoic, non-emotional (except at sporting events) always in control, always the problem solvers and never shedding tears, then it is no wonder that in this "Bush whacked" society we are suffering from performance anxiety" (Jackson, 2004).

Malidome Some, the African scholar of the Dagara People, suggests that there is a strong desire in young black men to, like other indigenous African cultures, for rituals or initiation to help them understand the reality in which they are living. In America, our rituals of manhood are "created in void initiations that are far more painful than anything else (gangs, and/or elitist groups that out-white white folks)." Some go on to suggest that black men free themselves from that which stops them from coming together to uplift each other and help develop strong, confident, creative black men and families.

Good news about Black men

There is good news about Black men. There are 484,000 Black men who are single parents. As of May 2010, there were 816,000 African American males in a school of higher learning. Two-thirds of black men in a survey conducted by the Washington Post, the Henry J. Kaiser Family Foundation, and Harvard University said they prayed at least once a day, a much higher percentage than white men (Holmes and Morin, 2006).

Calling the church back to men

"For years we have called men back to church. The time has come to call the church back to the men."(Vaughn, 2006). Black churches need not expect to see an increase in the attendance of Black men as long as the pastor focuses on messages of comfort or messages condemning the males. Given the state of the black man in America that include a large number of men in prisons or jails, or those who are the victims of some violent crime, or lost to alcohol and drugs, or struggling with racial injustices, it would seem that these men would make for a plentiful harvest for a church really seeking souls. It is sad to think that because a church can survive without actively seeking these troubled males thanks to the women, children, and few men who keep the doors open with their financial contributions that the church may not seek these men, at all. Dr. Martin Luther King Jr. in his "Letter from a Birmingham Jail," wrote that the church was in danger of being "dismissed as an irrelevant social club. In deep disappointment, I have wept over the laxity of the church ..., but be assured that my tears have been tears of love. There can be no deep disappointment where there is not deep love. Yes, I love the church" (King, 1963).

CHAPTER VIII

BLACK MEN JOIN LIBERATION CHURCHES, MEGA CHURCHES OR THE NATION OF ISLAM

The right questions need to be asked. It is important to note that, for the overwhelming majority of these men, non-attendance does not reflect irreligiosity and does not mean that Black men are not spiritual. The question that must be asked is where do Black men worship? According to Kunjufu, (1997) Black men join liberation churches, mega churches and the Nation of Islam. Lincoln and Mamiya (1990) posits that more men are affiliated with the Nation of Islam than women.

Liberation churches

There are a few Black churches in the United States that have had or currently have active programs that attract Black males. President Obama's former church, Trinity United Church of Christ, Chicago, Illinois is an African American mega church that adheres to a liberation theology. Jeremiah Wright, former pastor of Trinity United Church of Christ, believes that a church is not serious about Black theology until the members go beyond having a ministry to the poor, but making the members of the congregation equals (Wright, 2004). Trinity is best known today for its national and international social programs on behalf of the poor, albeit in its earliest days such outreach was not a feature of the its mission (Speller, 2005). Anthony Pinn of Rice University notes that Trinity United Church of Christ has 70 ministries with social justice advocacy at the core of its theological perspective. These are ministries that help the poor, the unemployed, those with AIDS or those in prison (Hagerty, 2008). Men who become a part of Trinity United Church of Christ have the opportunity to become a part of Men's ministries where men serve together and grow together. Prayer cells, an exhilarating and exceptional Men's Chorus, youth support and brotherhood are all included in these ministries (Speller, 2005; Wright, 2004).

Liberation is one of the major themes of the Bible. James Cone, the father of Black Liberation Theology based a great deal of his liberationist theology on God's deliverance of Israel from oppression under the Egyptians. The unswerving theme in Israelite history is God's concern for the denial of social, economic, and political justice for those who are poor and discarded in the society (Cone, 1990). Jesus launched his ministry by declaring that he had arrived to release the oppressed. Scripture teaches that Christ brings emancipation from slavery to sin, but it also reveals deliverance from corporeal forms of oppression. By becoming poor and entrusting divine revelation to a carpenter from Nazareth, God makes clear where one has to be in order to hear the divine word and experience divine presence (Cone, 1986). By rejecting white theology as heresy, the proponents of Black theology created a new theology of the Black poor, one that would empower them in their struggle for justice" (Cone, 1986). It teaches that the Black church must act on a new agenda. A constructive and practical Black Theology must emerge out of a "day-to-day struggle to survive, develop, and progress in an often hostile, uncaring, majority-dominated society (Foster and Smith, 2003).

Mega churches

A megachurch is simply a Protestant church that averages at least two thousand total attendees in their weekend services (Thumma and Travis, 2007). Contemporary Black megachurches have the best gospel music, and the greatest biblically based preaching to be heard. Additionally, the buildings and grounds are well kept, therefore Black men are not embarrassed to invite their friends to worship with them. Most Black megachurches offer a high measure of assertion of a Black identity in an unsympathetic white society (Gilkes, 1998). The function of worship in these African American mega-churches serves more than the customary commemorative purpose. The worship is about expectations, formulation for volunteerism, and a particular kind of lifestyle outside of the church walls (Barnes, 2010; Jackson, 2012). Comparable to Liberation Churches, some mega churches have as many as 100 programs and ministries, including homeless assistance, HIV and substance abuse counseling, bereavement services, and support for single adults (Ebony, 2004). Outreach is an indication that the church is relevant to the community and these types of activities attract Black men.

A few Black mega churches in addition to Trinity United Church of Christ currently have active programs seeking to reach Black males. They are Oak Cliff Bible Fellowship, Oak Cliff, Texas; and St. Paul Community Baptist Church, Brooklyn, New York.

Evans (2012), pastor of Oak Cliff Bible Fellowship of Dallas, Texas, exerts great effort in building what he calls Kingdom Men. Kingdom Men recognize that God has uniquely endowed them with the capacity and destiny for greatness. Evans says the time for the return of Kingdom Men has never been more critical. Our families need them. Our neighborhoods need them. Our churches need them. Our world needs them.

St. Paul Community Baptist Church of Brooklyn, New York, is currently pastored by David K. Brawley. However, Reverend Johnny Youngblood is credited with starting an incredible ministry to men which the church still maintains. In an interview with Peay (2005), Youngblood said that he changed the equation of St. Paul by visualizing men as natural leaders and encouraged them to use their spiritual gifts in the church. He also helped them mentor young Black males (Peay, 2005).

Nation of Islam

The Nation of Islam represents a serious threat to the Christian community. The Black Muslims (the Nation of Islam), the largest indigenous population of Americans who have become Muslims, filled a void in the Black religious experience (Lincoln and Mamiya 1990. Not only are they encouraging young Black males to join the Nation of Islam, but they are recruiting them from prisons, universities and Christian churches (Buckner, 2009; King, 2005; Zoba, 2000). Members of the Nation of Islam reached out to Black churches and recruited Black men by engaging in a practice called "fishing," where they stand outside Black Christian congregations as the Sunday service ends, criticizing church members about the inconsistencies of Christianity in white America (Gilkes, 1998). The composition of African American religion became so gendered that Lincoln and Mamiya (1990) point to the phenomenon of more Black males preferring Islam while more Black females adhere to traditional Black Christianity as a serious challenge facing the Black church. The role of protector as taught by the Nation of Islam is attractive to Black men (Mondesir, 2015). Black males get their needs met in the Nation of Islam. The Black male needs money, job opportunities, business resources, and relevant skills training. The church collects money, but the Nation of Islam teaches men how to make money. They urge Blacks to set up Black owned and Black operated businesses (Pement, 1997). The Nation of Islam places emphasis on eating better, avoiding drugs, alcohol, and smoking. They are known for cleaning up the ghettos and slums by getting rid of drug pushers, prostitutes, and other undesirable components in the community. The Nation of Islam emphasizes a strong family structure, and they affirm men by putting emphasis on fatherhood and Black manhood (Buckner, 2009). The above listed characteristics and activities are attractive to Black men.

According to a major survey done by the Pew Research Center and released in the spring of 2007, most of the Muslims who were born in the United States are African American converts and descendants of converts. If the conversion rate continues unchanged, Islam could become the dominant religion in Black urban areas by the year 2020 (Pipes, 2002).

CHAPTER IX

WHAT BLACK MEN NEED

Men are looking for relevance

Men have been complaining for years that the church is not relevant to them. It is not addressing the issues they face. A recent survey showed that 92% of churchgoing men have never heard a sermon on the subject of work. Is what a man does for most of the week not relevant to what a man does on Sabbath or Sunday mornings?

Men want to be involved in a cause greater than themselves. Making it in the workforce is nothing compared to what the church is called to do. The church has the mission to help save souls for eternity. Men are not going to give up their time, money, and energy to move papers around or attend "social" committee meetings. They want to be about the work of kingdom expansion.

Men want a shot at success. Men want to win. They want to be heroes. They want to come in first. Unfortunately, it seems that the church today wants nice men, not great men. How do we equip men to win at life? One thing the church can do is to encourage the men. When they take a step to faith, when they say NO to sin, when they serve effectively, say THANKS! Next, if we give them a vision for what they can become then we show them what greatness looks like in the eyes of God. They need a model or picture of it. The church needs to discuss it, imagine it, make it as concrete as possible. Then the men are ready to be released to fulfill that vision.

Men want to be challenged

It is part of a man's nature to view the world around them as something to overcome or conquer. Consider the simple task of shopping. For women, shopping is an experience; for men it is a challenge. For men it's usually a matter of spending the least amount of time finding it, buying it, and getting home. Again, men want to be challenged.

There are two ways to challenge men that need to be discussed here. The first way is to raise the standard of what is expected. Raise the bar on what you expect when it comes to leadership development, leading teams, and what it means to be a leader. Second, make the "Big Ask." A few years ago, at the Willow Creek leadership summit, Bill Hybels said one quality of a good leader is his ability to make the "Big Ask." This may require you to step out of your comfort zone to ask men to give more, serve more, and lead more. What I have discovered is that men are just waiting to be challenged and asked.

Incredible as it may seem men today are looking for something to do. Churches need to build opportunities into their ministries for men to serve outside the church walls. Get them involved in community activities like Habitat for Humanity, rescue missions, tutoring and/mentoring youths, or fix-it projects for widows in your area. Lasana Omar Hotep writes "black males need to stop thinking of divinity as limited to the confines of a building, stop building their faith on fear of damnation; and stop seeking personal salvation above the good of the whole" (Powell, 2008).

Men are looking for leaders and want to be leaders

It has been said that men do not follow programs, they follow men. Why, for example, do men go to Georgetown? Because they want to play for John Thompson. Why do men want to work for certain companies? Because of the reputation of the leader of that company. It is no different in the church. Men are attracted to strong masculine leadership and the church needs to provide it. They want to follow a bold, courageous, visionary leader. There is no other way to say it. Not only are men looking for a leader to follow, they want to become leaders themselves. They want to lead in their family, workplace, church, community, and world. One of the things you can do is equip them to lead. So often we tell them to lead their families, but we do not show them how nor empower them to do it.

Men are looking to have fun

The world is a serious place. Men are looking to laugh and have fun to balance that reality (Sonderman, 2008). A Monday Night Men's Group, for instance, could be a bridge builder and point of easy communication between Christians and non-Christians. It would be non-threatening and work on minimal content except at the meal table. Men's breakfasts have been a very successful way of bringing men together for mutual support and encouragement.

Men are looking for brothers

Most men have lots of acquaintances, but very few have a good friend. According to statistics, the average man over 35 years old does not have one close friend. They do not have models of what good friendships look like. Therefore, they are not equipped to make and/or grow deep friendships. It is the responsibility of the church to foster a place where healthy male friendships are modeled.

Men are looking to heal the father wound

We all come into the world powerless, dependent and needing approval, to be treated as worthy, and to be blessed. The father wound is the nonattendance of this love from your birth father. (Davis, 2008). No grief strikes more acutely into a man's heart than being neglected emotionally and/or physically by his father. No pain, therefore, more directly attracts the saving power of God the Father. That's why God's eschatological vision focuses directly on healing it–as in Malachi 4:5,6 NIV, I will send you the prophet Elijah before that great and dreadful day of the Lord comes. He will turn the hearts of the fathers to their children, and the hearts of the children to their fathers; or else I will come and strike the land with a curse (Dalbey, 2012). Richard Innes, (2012) declares no woman or mother can ever make a boy or a man love himself as a man.

The injury can be caused by copious reasons, including but not limited to neglect – I am unimportant; absence – divorce, separation, death; abuse – mental, physical, sexual, spiritual; control – overbearing; lack of blessings – at various stages of life; and lack of confirmation – that leads to a lack of self-acceptance. The effect of a father wound is low self-worth, deep emotional harm and a performance point of reference that makes us doers rather than beings. While salvation makes us new creatures in Christ, it does not necessarily address this wound inside.

Robert M. Lewis (2005) in Men's Fraternity: Quest for Authentic Manhood emphasize five common wounds that are in most men today. Five wounds men must deal with:

1. The absent father wound - A father who was never there, or a father who was physically there but wasn't there.
2. The overly bonded with mother wound (apron) - Mom, for whatever reason, invested too strongly in you. Compensated for a missing dad and she overly controlled you and nurtured you and touched your world too much. She bonded with you too deeply and took care of you too often.
3. The all alone wound (a rope) - We may have friends who are connected to our outer lives, but no close friends who have access to our inner lives. Our ropes are cut. When we go through turmoil (support and counsel) we have no one to talk to, we do it alone. We have no friends who can cheer (encouragement) for us in the noble things of life. No one where we can share in our victories and accomplishments and get the encouragement we need to continue on. We have no friends who can help us have a broader, clearer

perspective on life, so we doom ourselves to "blind spots". No one in your life that is allowed to help deliver you from a circle of doom – to tell you when you are heading down a wrong path or making poor, ungodly decisions and choices.
4. The lack of a manhood vision wound. (binoculars) - You have not vision of who you want to be. Your life consists of the "living in the now". Your vision goes to next week or the weekend. The world offers a short-sighted vision of manhood, a *"conventional vision of manhood"*. This tells a young man that if you put on a Warrior face, if you work really hard, even if it hurts your marriage and family, but if you sacrifice and work really hard, eventually you will have all you need, and you will not need anybody. You will be alone, but happy and satisfied. The truth is that the "conventional vision of manhood" is a lie. It will not to take anyone to Authentic Masculinity.
5. The heart wound (sin) – this is not a wound of nurture, it is a wound of our nature. Everyone has this wound; it is in our nature. Romans 7 Why do I feel a pull to do evil? Why do I feel that I do not have the power to overcome it, to do the thing are right? Why do I keep doing the things I know will hurt my family? Why am I out of control? Where do I find the power to do what is right? The list goes on. This is a wound of the soul and spirit that no counselor can fix. This wound requires a deeper answer and that answer is Jesus. Jesus alone has the answer to the wound of sin. Until addressed, this wound will continually undercut your masculinity.

We tend to have at a minimum four barriers that inhibit the healing of this wound and they are as follows: pride – no will to face up to or change – "I'm alright", sin – no will to confess or receive forgiveness, the wound itself – emotional damage inside, and lies – misconceptions about self, birth father and our heavenly Father. Until these wounds and hurts are dealt with in a healthy way, they will never become the man that God intends them to be.

There are several things the church can do to create an environment that is practical about healing: Provide support groups where men feel free to share their wounds and deal with them; offer men's fraternity to men to deals with these specific issues; bring these issues up in small group or preaching ministry and address them for the whole church.

Last, but not least, men are looking for accountability

One of the reasons why the nation of Israel wandered in the desert for forty years is because men refused to listen to each other. Men do not want to rely on anyone else for anything. If you view accountability as that which takes place when men get together and are honest with each other about their struggles and shortfalls; pray together, and for each other, then the church is an ideal place to meet. Brothers aim toward becoming more Christlike. Each one is encouraged to reach their fullest potential as a man of God. All of this would take place in an atmosphere of love and acceptance and without judgment. "How good and pleasant it is, when brothers live together in unity" (Psalms 133:1). The Bible is filled with examples of vital relationships among great men of God.

> "Moses had Aaron. David had Jonathan. Paul had Silas, Timothy and Titus, to name a few. Jesus had the twelve, and an even closer relationship with Peter, James, and John. They did not try to go it alone. One of the great benefits of accountability is that you will look at your life more closely than ever before" (McGee 2010).

Develop a healthy masculine spirit in your church

Want to attract men to church? Cultivate an environment that makes them feel welcomed, needed, and wanted. Few men would feel comfortable spending their Sabbath mornings in places of worship that feel more like a ladies' club, with the pastor catering solely to women's needs at the expense of men's. When you examine the facts, you will find that the overwhelming message communicated to men is the reason God put them on earth is to be a "good boy." A man's spirit is mortally wounded when he continues to hear the message that the greatest achievement of his life is to not offend anyone, don't rock the boat, and whatever you do don't take risks.

Men are designed to take risks. They like adventure, danger, and exploration. Look at the kind of games men like to play. If you ask men to list their favorite movies you will probably find *The Shawshank Redemption*, *Die Hard* series, *Shaft*, etc. on their list.

> "Our culture has latched onto images of God as male and then defined for us what male means. Male means winning (being number 1 in sports, business, politics, academia), going to war ("kill or be killed"), being rational, not emotional ("boys don't cry"), and embracing homophobia (fear of male affection). Male means domination, lording over others-whether nature, one's own body, women or others" (Fox, 2008).

Make no mistake about it – aggression is in all of us to some degree. Instead of concentrating on the negative ways in which aggression expresses itself we need to look for healthy ways to engage it. A relationship with Christ enables men to turn aggression into nobility.

Promote Christ's masculine side

For too many years pastors have focused on Christ's tenderness and empathy. This is not a bad thing, however only portraying Jesus as a soft-spoken, mild mannered guy week after week can turn men off. Christ has been called "The Lion of the tribe of Judah." The book of Revelation reveals that when Christ returns, He will be riding a white horse with his robe dipped in blood. He is not sweet, but He is loving. We also know Christ as being immensely brave and fierce. "Men are made to take risks and live passionately on behalf of others" (Eldredge, 2001).

Shun feminine terminology

Words like precious, share, and relationship are generally words, that men do not use regularly. Words like saved and lost aren't exactly words men consider masculine, either. Many are confused by the message that they are to develop a personal relationship with Jesus. Christ's bold masculine command, "Follow Me!" is now, "Have a nice relationship with Me." To top it off, many of the words in contemporary songs emphasize the church as the bride of Christ, thus emphasizing the believer's role as the receiver in the relationship (a feminine position much like the wife in a marriage) instead of balancing out the songs with hymns and lyrics that emphasize Christ as King and His church as His army called forth to conquer the nations for Him (Creation Tips, 2009).

Preach shorter sermons

Many pastors may not like the idea of preaching shorter sermons, but many men have said that one of the reasons why they refuse to go to church is the long, boring sermon they are expected to sit through. Thanks to today's technology the attention span of men has dwindled considerably. It would seem that the opportunity to preach a sermon that quickly expounds on the main theme would be advantageous to the church, especially the men. Keep in mind that Jesus' most beloved lessons were his parables, none of which took more than a couple of minutes to teach. His parables survive today because men remembered them and wrote them in the Bible.

Develop into students of men

Most pastors are male. Most members of their congregations are female. Therefore, most pastors are preaching to what makes the women in their congregations happy and keeps them volunteering. If we want more men to come to church this must change. Men need to learn about men. John Eldredge's bestseller *Wild at Heart, explains* that "men long for freedom and passion; they long for a cause, a battle; they long for an adventure with a beauty. They cannot be happy without those things."

Twelve Marks of a Man-Friendly Church

David Murrow (2008) expounds on twelve characteristics of a man-friendly church in his book How Women Help Men Find God. Murrow inculcates the idea that you are more likely to find excited men in churches that conform to the following twelve characteristics:

1. Men prefer large churches
2. Men prefer nondenominational churches
3. Men prefer adherence to scripture
4. Men gravitate toward a young, multiracial crowd
5. Men prefer churches that are themselves young (recently founded)
6. Men look for energized men
7. Men like manly pastors who project a healthy masculinity
8. Men are drawn to quality, but not excessive showy-ness
9. Men like "come as you are" churches
10. Men like modern technology
11. Men like churches that aren't afraid to have a few laughs
12. Men like churches that have a clear, unique vision and mission

As a Rule, Men are Different from Women

Men	Women
1. Chauvinistic, cold logic	More emotional
2. Work oriented	Relationship oriented
3. Goal oriented	Enjoy the detailed process
4. Learn by analysis	Know intuitively
5. Physically strong	Physically weaker
6. Often feel inadequate	Most often to feel depressed
7. Can only cope with one issue at a time	Able to appreciate past, present, and future

While the world of science is often used to avoid confronting God it generally can be found to consistently confirm biblical precepts. This is also true regarding differences between the sexes.

1. Women have a greater sense of relationship. A characteristic which colors a woman's whole life.
2. She has a greater need for conversation in creating and understanding relationships. Meanwhile men talk simply to solve problems at which point conversation ends.
3. Women see a greater need for dependence between people while men see people as independent or self-reliant.
4. Women emphasize caring while men value separation and freedom.
5. Women assess actions within a context, as one aspect of the detail of the whole–linking each action. Men often regard events in isolation (Lien of OZ, 2012)

Generate a culture of person-to-person challenge

While it is true that many pastors will issue challenges to their congregations from the pulpit, the members don't challenge each other. " Person-to –person discipleship, in small teams, is the only way to bring men to maturity in

Christ" (Morrow, 2005). We have the example that Jesus left us to follow. Take a handful of men and personally disciple them, with the understanding that each man will, in turn, disciple his own small group. Continue to work with your original group after they have started discipling their own. This model is what Jesus used. It is not restricted for use with men only. If the church is truly going to follow Christ's lead, then both men and women need to work together.

E. G. White wrote in her book *Education:*

> "The greatest want of the world is the want of men-men who will not be bought or sold, men who in their inmost souls are true and honest, men who do not fear to call sin by its right name, men whose conscience is as true to duty as the needle to the pole, men who will stand for the right though the heavens fall" (p. 57)

Jesus is still calling men to take up the cross and follow His lead. This responsibility also requires men to lead their families through love and strength, in the ministry of the church. All other ministries will follow if men allow God to make them spiritually strong through prayer, repentance, forgiveness, and humble obedience.

Hints for inviting men to church

What, then, is the most effective way to reach people, especially African American men today? The Institute for American Church Growth asked over 10,000 people this question:

"What was responsible for your coming to Christ and this church?"

1. I had a special need   1%
2. I just walked in   3%
3. I liked the minister   6%

4.	I visited there	1%
5.	I liked the Bible classes	5%
6.	I attended a gospel meeting	0.5%
7.	I liked the programs	3%
8.	A friend or relative invited me	79%

According to the responses we see that we all have work to do to get those people we know invited to church. One of the first things we need to do is to make a list to help us focus our attention upon those we hope to reach for the Lord. Of course, we should start with those who are closest to us and work outwardly.

When making "The List" be sure to include your family, friends, co-workers, neighbors, relatives of fellow church members, regular visitors to the services of the church, and last, but not least casual acquaintances like the mailman, store clerks, etc. Second, limit this list to five, but no more than eight souls (a list with too many and you will not be able to focus your efforts effectively). Next you should give priority to those who are the "unchurched." These are the people that you know that are not active members of any denomination or particular religion. This group may include those who are active members of a denomination or religion who are often very satisfied with their human traditions, but who must be taught the simple truths of the gospel.

Husbands and wives should probably have one list. This will require joint cooperation. You can make one list together or make two separate lists and then prayerfully develop one list.

Finally, keep this list where you will see it daily. Keeping the list in sight will constantly serve as a reminder of these people, and help you as you follow the next steps.

Pray for those on your list daily. It is God who gives the increase when it comes to evangelism. "I have planted, Apollos watered; but God gave the increase. So then neither is he that planteth anything neither he that watereth; but God that giveth the increase" (I Corinthians 3: 6,7). We are servants whom God can use in His providential workings. "...so though we may work as though it all depends upon us, let us pray as though it all depends upon God" (I Corinthians 3:5).

Our prayers should be a request to God that he will work together with us to give opportunities to do good for those on our list and the wisdom to make the most of those opportunities. Our prayers should also include a request for boldness to say what needs to be said at the proper time.

To those on "The List" we pray that they will have the opportunity to hear the truth and have the open hearts they need to receive it. While we are praying for them, we should also demonstrate our love for them.

It has been said that people don't really care how much you know until they know how much you care. A demonstration of love will make a person more likely to be receptive to the gospel of love when it is shared (See I Peter 2:12).

By observing the good works that we do they will see an example of how to glorify God through joyful obedience. Love and good works will help prepare the "soil" to be as receptive as possible when the "seed" is finally sown.

There are several things we can do to put our good works into action. We can invite our future friends in Christ to our homes for a meal. We can and should visit them, especially in times of trial or sickness. Last, but not least, we should do some things with them on a social level. Hospitality and neighborliness will go a long way to increase opportunities to share the gospel. When people see the incarnation of the gospel (the principles of the gospel lived in out in the flesh), they will be more likely to believe in the truth of the gospel in spoken or written word.

> "Christ's method alone will give true success in reaching the people. The Savior mingled with men as one who desired their good. He showed His sympathy for men, ministered to their needs, and won their confidence. Then he bade them, '"Follow Me'" (Ellen G. White, *Ministry of Healing*, p. 143).

REFERENCES

Adams, G. R. and Schvaneveldt, J. D., 1991. *Understanding Research methods*. 2nd ed. London: Longman.

Ahlstrom, S. E., 1972. *A religious history of the American people*. New Haven and London: Yale University Press.

Akerlof, G. A., Yellen, J. L., and Katz, M. L., 1996. An analysis of out-of-wedlock childbearing in the United States. *The Quarterly Journal of Economics*, 111(2), pp. 277–317.

Alexander, M., 2010. *The new jim crow: Mass incarceration in the age of colorblindness*. New York: The New Press.

Ali, C., 1999. *Survival and liberation: Pastoral theology in African American context*. Chalice Press.

Assensoh, Y. A. and Assensoh, A. B., 2001. Inner-City contexts, church attendance, and African-American political participation. *The Journal of Politics*, 63(3), pp. 886-901.

Auerbach, C. F. and Silverstein, L. B., 2003. *Qualitative data: An introduction to coding and analysis*. New York: New York University Press.

Aune, K., 2008. Evangelical Christianity and women's changing lives. *European Journal of Women's Studies*, 15(3), pp. 277-294.

Bacchus, N. A. and Holley, L. C., 2005. Spirituality as a coping resource. *Journal of Ethnic and Cultural Diversity in Social Work*, 13(4) pp. 65-84. Retrieved from http://dx.doi.org/10.1300/J051v13n04_04.

Bacon, H., 2012. Thinking the trinity as resource for feminist theology today? *Cross Currents*, 62(4), pp. 442-464.

Bader, C. D. and Desmond, S. A., 2006. Do as i say and as i do: The effects of consistent parental beliefs and behaviors upon religious transmission. *Sociology of Religion*, 67(3), pp. 313-329.

Bainbridge, W. S., 1989. The Religious Ecology of Deviance. American Sociological Review, 54, pp. 288-295.

Barna Research Group, 7 May 2007. The spirituality of moms outpaces that of dads. *The Barna Group*. https://www.barna.org/barna-update/family-kids/104-the...

Barna Research Group, 1 August 2015. 20 years of surveys show key differences in faith of America's men and women. *The Barna Group*. https://www.barna.org/barna-update/faith-spirituality/508-20-years...

Barna Research Group, 25 June 2015. Five factors changing women's relationship with churches. *The Barna Group*. https://www.barna.org/barna-update/culture/722-five-factors...

Barna Research Group, 16 March 2017. The credibility crisis of today's pastors. Retrieved from https://www.barna.com/research/credibility-crisis-todays-pastors/.

Barnes, S. L., 2005. Black church culture and community action. *Social Forces*, 84(2) pp. 967-994.

Barnes, S. L., 2010. *Black megachurch culture: Models for education and empowerment.* New York: Peter Lang Publishing Inc.

Berger, P. L., 1967. *The Sacred Canopy.* New York, NY: Anchor Books.

BlackandChristian.com, 2017. Retrieved from http://www.blackandchristian.com/blackchurch/index.shtml.

Blair, L., 13 July 2016. Megachurch pastor Jamal Bryant says the church is failing Black lives matter. *Christian Post*. Retrieved from www.christianpost.com/news/megachurch-pastor-jamal-bryant-church-failing-black-lives-matter-166428/#IrUuxVtLSJblGWTo.99.

Brink, H., van der Walt, C. and van Rensburg, G., 2017. *Fundamentals of Research Methodology for Health Care Professionals.* 3rd edition. Africa: Juta and Company Ltd.

Brown, L., 26 October, 2005. There is an economic war on Black America. *The Norfolk Journal and Guide*.

Brown, R. K. and Brown, R. E., 2003. Faith and works: Church-based social capital resources and African American political activism. *Social Forces*, 82(2), pp. 617-641.

Bruce, R. and Bruce, D. F., 1996. *Becoming spiritual soulmates with your child*. Nashville: Broadman and Holman Publishers.

Bryant, A. N., 2007. Gender differences in spiritual development during the college years. *Sex Roles*, 56(11-12), pp. 835–846.

Buchko, K. J., 2004. Religious beliefs and practices of college women as compared to college men. *Journal of College Student Development*, 45, pp. 89–98.

Burgess, N. J. and Brown, E., 2000. *African American women: An ecological perspective*. New York: Palmer Press.

Butler-Ajibade, P., Booth, W. and Burwell, C., 2012. Partnering with the Black church: Recipe for promoting heart health in the stroke belt. *ABNF Journal*, pp. 34-37.

Carlton-LaNey, I., 2006. Mutual aid "doing the lord's work": African American elders' civic engagement. *Generations*, 30, pp. 47-50.

Carothers, S. S., Borkowski, J. G., Lefever, J. B. and Whitman, T. L., 2005. Religiosity and the socioemotional adjustment of adolescent mothers and their children. *Journal of Family Psychology*, 2005, 19(2), pp. 263–275.

Cartledge, M. L., 2003. *Practical theology: Charismatic and empirical perspectives*. Carlisle, Cumbria, UK: Paternoster Press.

Casanova, J., 2006. Rethinking secularization: A global comparative perspective. *The Hedgehog Review*, 8(1–2), pp. 7–22.

Chandler, D. J., 2017. African American spirituality: Through another lens. *Journal of Spiritual Formation and Soul Care*, 10(2), pp. 159-181.

Chavest, M. and Higginst, L. M., 1992. Comparing the community involvement of Black and white congregations. *Journal for the Scientific Study of Religion*, 31 (4) pp. 425-440.

Christ, C. P. and Plaskow, J., 2016. *Goddess and God in the world: Conversations in embodied theology*. Minneapolis: Fortress Press.

Clifton, S., 2009. *Pentecostal churches in transition: Analysing the developing ecclesiology of the assemblies of god in Australia. Global Pentecostal and Charismatic Studies, 3.* Leiden; Boston: Brill Publishers.

Coats, C., 2009. God, man, then ...wait, how does that go? Emerging gender identities in 20-something evangelicals. *Journal of Men, Masculinities and Spirituality,* 3(1), pp. 64-79. London: Routledge Falmer.

Cohen, L., Manion, L. and Morrison, K., 2007. *Research methods in education.* 6th ed.London: Routledge Falmer.

Coleman, S., 2000. *The globalization of charismatic Christianity: Spreading the gospel of prosperity.* Cambridge University Press.

Coley, R.L. and Medeiros, B.L., 2007. Reciprocal longitudinal relations between nonresident father involvement and adolescent delinquency. *Child Development,* 78, pp. 132-147.

Collett, J. and Lizardo, O., 2009. A power-control theory of gender and religiosity. *Journal for the Scientific Study of Religion,* 48(2), pp. 213-231.

Collier-Thomas, B., 1998. *Daughters of thunder: Black women preachers and their sermons, 1850-1979.* San Francisco, Calif: Jossey-Bass.

Comminey, S., 1999. The society for the propagation of the gospel in foreign parts and Black education in South Carolina, 1702-1764. *The Journal of Negro History,* 84(4), pp. 360-369.

Cone, J. H., 1986. *Speaking the truth: Ecumenism, liberation, and Black theology.* Maryknoll, New York: Orbis Books.

Cone, J. H., 1990. *A theology of Black liberation, twentieth anniversary edition.* Maryknoll, New York: Orbis Books.

Craven, S. M., 19 June 2011. Fathers: Key to their children's faith. *Christian Post.* Retrieved from www.christianpost.com > opinion.

Creswell, J. W., 1998. *Qualitative inquiry and research design: Choosing among five traditions.* Thousand Oaks, CA: Sage.

Cultwatch, n. d. How pastors get rich. Retrieved from www.cultwatch.com.

Davis, R. F., 2013. *The Black church: Relevant or irrelevant in the 21st century?* Macon, Georgia: Smyth and Helwys.

Day, A., 2008. Wilfully disempowered. *European Journal of Women's Studies,* 15(3), pp. 261 –276.

Denzin, N. and Lincoln, Y. (Eds.), 2005. *Handbook of qualitative research*, 3rd ed. Thousand Oaks, CA: Sage.

DeVaus, D., 1984. Workforce participation and sex differences in church attendance. *Review of Religious Research*, 25, pp. 247-256.

DeVaus, D. and McAllister, I., 1987. Gender differences in religion: A test of the structural location theory. *American Sociological Review*, 52(4), pp. 472-481.

Dictionary.com. 2016. Retrieved from http://www.dictionary.com/

Dixon, P., 2009. Marriage among African Americans: What does the research reveal? *Journal of African American Studies*, 13, pp. 29-46.

Dubois, W. E. B., 1903. *The Negro church*. Atlanta, Ga: The Atlanta University Press.

Ebony, December 2004. Mega churches: Large congregations spread across Black America.

Edgell, P., 2013. *Religion and family in a changing society*. Princeton University Press.

Eldredge, J., 2001. Wild at heart: Discovering the secret of a man's soul. Nashville: Thomas Nelson.

Ellis, L., Hoskin, A. and Ratnasingam, M., 2016. Testosterone, risk taking, and religiosity: Evidence from two cultures. *Journal for the Scientific Study of Religion*, 55(1), pp. 153-173.

Ellison, C. G., and Anderson, K. L., 2001. Religious involvement and domestic violence among U.S. couples. *Journal for the Scientific Study of Religion*, 40, pp. 269-286.

Evans, C., 2007. W. E. B. Du Bois Interpreting religion and the problem of the Negro church. *Journal of the American Academy of Religion*, 75(2), pp. 268-297.

Evans, T., 2012. *Kingdom man*. Nashville, TN: LifeWay.

Fenn, R. K., 2003. *The Blackwell companion to sociology of religion*. Malden, Mass: Blackwell.

Field, C., 1993. Adam and Eve: Gender in English free church constituency. *Journal of Ecclesiastical History*, 44(1) pp. 63-79.

Fitzgerald, S.T. and Spohn, R. E., 2005. Pulpits and platforms: The role of the church in determining protest among Black Americans. *Social Forces*, 84(2), pp. 1015-1048.

Foster, C. R. and Smith, F., 2003. Black religious experience: Conversations on doubt- consciousness and the work of Grant Shocktey. Nashville, TN: Abingdon.

Francis, L. J., 1997. The psychology of gender differences in religion: A review of empirical research, religion, 27, pp. 81-96, DOI: 10.1006/reli.1996.0066. http://dx.doi.org/10.1006/reli.1996.0066.

Frazier, E. F., 1964. *The Negro church in America*. Schocken Books.

Frost, J. and Edgell, P., 2017. Distinctiveness reconsidered: religiosity, structural location, and understandings of racial inequality. *Journal for the Scientific Study of Religion*, 56(2), pp. 277-301.

Furious, 14 May 2013. Black churches have collected $420 billion? Urban Intellectuals. Retrieved from http://urbanintellectuals.com/2013/05/14/black-churches-have...

Gallup, 11 July 2001. Race and social audit. Retrieved from http://www.gallup.com/poll/4627/Gallup-Social-Audit-BlackWhite-Relations-US.aspx.

Gallup, 2002. Why are women more religious? Retrieved from www.gallup.com/poll/7432/Why-Women-More-Religious.aspx.

Gilkes, C. T., 1998. Plenty good room: Adaptation in a changing Black church. *The Annals of the American Academy of Political and Social Science*, 558, pp. 101-121.

Gilkes, C. T., 2001. *If it wasn't for the women: Black women's experience and womanist culture in church and community*. Maryknoll: Orbis Books.

Gillum, T. L., 2009. The intersection of spirituality, religion and intimate partner violence in the African American community. *Institute on Domestic Violence in the African American Community*. Retrieved from http://www.idvaac.org/media/pubs/TheIntersectionofSpirituality.pdf

Glick, P. C. (ed.), McAdoo, H. P., 1997. *Black families* (3rd ed.). Thousand Oaks, Calif: Sage.

Goldenberg, N., 1979. *The changing of the gods: Feminism and the end of traditional religions.* Boston: Beacon.

Grove, S. K., Gray, J. R. and Burns, N., 2015. *Understanding Nursing Research: Building an evidence-based practice.* 6th edition. China: Elsevier.

Hagerty, B. B., 18 March 2008. A closer look at Black liberation theology. NPR. Retrieved from http://www.npr.org/templates/story/story.php?storyId=88512189.

Hall, L., 1997. *The religious and social consciousness of African-American baptist women.* Diss., Princeton University.

Hampson, D., 1990. *Theology and feminism.* Oxford: Blackwell.

Harrell, D. E., 1975. *All things are possible: The healing and charismatic revivals in modern America.* Indiana University Press.

Harris, F. C., 2001. *Black churches and civic traditions: Outreach activism, and the politics of public funding of faith-based ministries.* Can Charitable Choice Work? Covering Religion's Impact on Urban Affairs and Social Services; Edited by Andrew Walsh. Hartford: Pew Program on Religion and the News Media and the Leonard E. Greenberg Center for the Study of Religion in Public Life, 2001, pp. 140–156. Retrieved from http://www.trincoll.edu/depts/csrpl/Charitable%20Choice%20book/contents.htm.

Harris, F. C., Summer 2015. The next civil rights movement? *Dissent.* Retrieved from https://franklinhslibrary.pbworks.com/w/file/fetch/101640115/Black%20Lives%20Matter.pdf.

Hattery, A. J. and Smith, E., 2007. *African American families.* Thousand Oaks, Calif.: Sage.

Haug, W. and Wanner, P., 2000. *The demographic characteristics of linguistic and religious groups in Switzerland.* The Demographic Characteristics of National Minorities in Certain European States. *Population Studies, 31(2).* Germany: Council of Europe.

Hertel, B. R. and Donahue, M. J., 1995. Parental influences on God images among children: Testing durkheim's metaphoric parallelism. *Journal for the Scientific Study of Religion,* 34, pp. 186–199.

Higginbotham, E. B., 1993. *Righteous discontent: The women's movement in the Black baptist church, 1880-1920.* Cambridge: Harvard University Press.

Hirschle, J., 2013. "Secularization of consciousness" or alternative opportunities? The impact of economic growth on religious belief and practice in 13 European countries. *Journal for the Scientific Study of Religion,* 52(2), pp. 410-424.

Hodges, T. L., Rowland, M. L. and Isaac-Savage, E., 2016. Black males in black churches. *New Directions for Adult and Continuing Education,* 216(150), pp. 47-57. doi:10.1002/ace.20185.

Horner, B., Ralston, R. and Sunde, D., December 1996. *The promise keeper at work: Promise builders study series.* Focus on the Family Publishing.

House, H. W., 1982. An investigation of Black liberation theology. *Bibliotheca Sacra,* 139.

House, P., 2003. Want your church to grow? Then bring in the men. *Baptist Press.* Retrieved from www.bpnews.net/bpnews.asp?ID=15630.

Howe, E. M., 1979. *The positive case for the ordination of women,* In perspectives on evangelical theology, eds. Kantzer, K. S. and Gundry, S. N. Grand Rapids: Baker Book House.

Jackson, E. R., 2012. Black megachurch culture. *The Journal of Pan African Studies,* 5(1).

Jansen, H., 2010. The logic of qualitative survey research and its position in the field of social research methods [63 paragraphs]. *Forum Qualitative Sozialforschung / Forum: Qualitative Social Research,* 11(2). Retrieved from http://nbn-resolving.de/urn:nbn:de:0114-fqs1002110.

Jenkins, P., 2006. *The new faces of Christianity: Believing the bible in the global south.* Oxford University Press.

Johnson, R., n. d. The pimping preacher. *Forgotten Word Ministries.* Retrieved from www.forgottenword.org/pimpingpreachers.html.

Johnston, L. D., O'Malley, P. M., Bachman, J. G., and Schulenberg, J. E., 2007. *Monitoring the future national survey results on drug use, 1975-2006, vol. 1, secondary school students.* U. S. Department of Health and

Human Services, National Institute of Drug Abuse, NIH Pub. No. 07-6205, Bethesda, Maryland.

Johnston, R., 1954. *The development of Negro religion*. New York: Philosophical Library.

Jones, C. C., 1842. *The religious instruction of the Negroes in the United States*. Savannah: Thomas Purse.

Jones, J. and Mosher, W. D., 20 December 2013. Fathers' involvement with their children: United States, 2006-2010. *National Health Statistics Report*, 71, pp. 1-21. Retrieved from http://www.cdc.gov/nchs/data/nhsr/nhsr071.pdf.

Kanak, M. and Arslan, A., 2018. Sexual abusers in the eyes of preschool teachers: A qualitative study. *Ekev Academic Review*, 22(73), pp. 345-365.

King, C. I., 20 August 2005. Muslim converts, meet FBI. *Washington Post*.

King, V., 2003. The influence of religion on fathers' relationships with their children. *Journal of Marriage and Family*, 65(2).

Kunjufu, K., 1997. *Adam! Where are you? Why most black men don't go to church*. Chicago: African American Images.

Lee, D., 5 July 2017. Single Mother Statistics, *Single Mother Guide*.

Leffingwell, C., 2012. Eternal insurance: No boys allowed! Understanding gender disparities in church attendance through a study of churches in Hartford, Connecticut. *Honors Scholar Theses*. Retrieved from 250. http://digitalcommons.uconn.edu/srhonors_theses/250.

Lester, D., 1987. Religiosity and Personal Violence: A Regional Analysis of Suicide and Homicide Rates. *The Journal of Social Psychology*, 127, pp. 685-686.

Lincoln, C. and Mamiya, L., 1990. *The Black church in the African-American experience*. Durham: Duke University Press.

Linton, J. and Mowat, H., 2006. *Qualitative research and practical theology*. London: SCM Press.

Littlefield, M. B., 2005. The Black church and community development and self-help: The next phase of social equality. *The Western Journal of Black Studies*, 29(4), pp. 687–693.

Livingston, G. and Parker, K., 15 June 2011. A tale of two fathers. *Pew Research Center*. Retrieved from http://www.pewsocialtrends.org/2011/06/15/a-tale-of-two-fathers/2/.

Lofquist, D., Lugaila, T., O'Connell, M. and Feliz, S., 2010. Households and families: 2010. *US Census Bureau*. Retrieved from http://www.census.gov/prod/cen2010/briefs/c2010br-14.pdf.

Low, R., June 2003. The truth about men and church. *Touchstone*, 16 (5). Retrieved from www.touchstonemag.com/archives/article.php?id=16-05-024-v.

Malterud, K., Siersmaa, V. D. and Guassora, A. D., 2016. Sample size in qualitative interview studies: Guided by information power. *Qualitative Health Research*, 26(13), pp. 1753-1760.

Marshall, C., 15 January 2016. Face-to-face interviews - Advantages and disadvantages. Retrieved from https://www.linkedin.com/pulse/face-to-face-interviews-advantages-disadvantages-charlie-marshall.

Martin, D., 2017. *On secularization: Towards a revised general theory*. London: Routledge.

Martin, M., 2013. Redefining philanthropy: How African-Americans give back. Retrieved from http://www.npr.org/2013/12/30/258382689/.

Mattis, J. S., 2002. Religion and spirituality in the meaning-making and coping experiences of African American women: A qualitative analysis. *Psychology of Women Quarterly*, 26, pp. 309-321.

Mattis, J., Eubanks, S., Zapata, A., Grayman, N., Belkin, M., Mitchell, N. and Cooper, S., 2004. *Factors influencing religious non-attendance among African American men: A multi-method analysis. Review of Religious Research*, 45, pp. 386-403.

McGee, P. L., 2017. *Brand® new theology: The wal-martization of t. d. jakes and the new ...* Maryknoll, New York: Orbis Books.

McIntosh, E., 2007. The possibility of a gender-transcendent God: Taking Macmurray forward. *The Journal of the Britain and Ireland School of Feminist Theology*, 15, pp. 236-255.

Mckenzie-Mohr, D. and Smith, W., 1999. *Fostering sustainable behavior: An introduction to community-based social marketing.* Gabriola Island, Canada: New Society Publishers.

McRae, B., 24 April 2012. Building a visitor friendly church. *Bible.org.* Retrieved from bible.org/article/building-visitor-friendly-<.

Mellowes, M., 2010. God in American: The Black church. www.pbs.org/godinamerica/black-church.

Merriam, S., 2009. *Qualitative research: A guide to design and implementation.* San Francisco, CA: Jossey-Bass.

Merrill, R. M., Salazar, R. D., and Gardner, N. W., 2001. Relationship between family religiosity and drug use behavior among youth. *Social Behavior and Personality,* 29, pp. 347–358.

Miller, A. S. and Stark, R., 2002. Gender and religiousness: Can socialization explanations be saved? *American Journal of Sociology,* 107, pp. 1399–1423.

Miller, S. I. and Fredericks, M., 2002. Naturalistic inquiry and reliabilism: A compatible epistemological grounding. *Qualitative Health Research,* 12(7), pp. 982-989.

Minton, T. D. and Zeng, Z., 2015. Jail inmates at midyear 2014. U.S. Department of Justice.

Mondesir, D. M., 21 August 2015. Will our Black men leave the church for the Nation of Islam? *The Gospel Herald.* Retrieved from http://www.gospelherald.com/articles/57303/20150821/will-our-black-men-leave-the-church-for-the-nation-of-islam.htm.

Montgomery, W. E., 1993. *Under their own vine and fig tree: The African-American church in the south, 1865-1900.* Baton Rouge, La: Louisiana State University.

Morley, P., 10 December 2008. How to reach men on the "fringe" through your church. *Man in the Mirror.* Retrieved from www.maninthemirror.org/a-look-in-the-mirror/38-how-to-reach-men-on-the-qfringeq-through-your-church.

Myrdal, G., 1971. *The Negro church in the Negro community.* The Black church in America. Editors Hart M. Nelsen, Raytha Yokley, and Anne K. Nelsen. New York: Basic Bocks, Inc.

Namageyo-Funa, A., Rimando, M., Brace, A. M., Christiana, R. W., Fowles, T. L., Davis, T. L., Martinez, L. M., and Sealy, D., 2014. Recruitment in Qualitative Public Health Research: Lessons Learned During Dissertation Sample Recruitment. *The Qualitative Report, 19*(4), pp. 1-17. Retrieved from http://nsuworks.nova.edu/tqr/vol19/iss4/3.

Neuman, W. L., 2006. *Social research method: Qualitative and quantitative approaches.* 6th ed. Boston: Pearson.

Nordling, C. F., 2005. *Feminist biblical interpretation", dictionary for theological interpretation of the bible*, ed. Van Hoozer, K. J. Grand Rapids, MI: Baker Academic.

Osmer, R. R., 2007. *Practical theology: An introduction.* Grand Rapids: Eerdmans.

Pace, E., 2017. Systems theory and religion. *Civitas, 17*(2), pp. 354-359.

Pembroke, N., 2011. Sacred Love Negotiations: A Qualitative Approach to Equality and Mutuality, and Negotiating Around Needs in Marriage and Family Life in the Experience of Australian Mainline Christians. *International Journal of Practical Theology, 15,* pp. 149–172.

Pement, E., 1997. Louis Farrakhan and the nation of Islam: Part one. *Cornerstone, 26*(111), pp. 10-16.

Petts, R. J., 2009a. Fathers' religious involvement and early childhood behavior. *Fragile Families Working Paper 209-22 FF.*

Pew Research Center, 22 May 2007. Muslim Americans: Middle class and mostly mainstream.

Pew Research Center, February 2008. U.S. religious landscape survey. Retrieved from http://religions.pewforum.org/pdf/report-religious-landscape-study-full.pdf.

Pew Research Center, 30 January 2009. A religious portrait of African-Americans. Retrieved from www.pewforum.org/2009/01/30/a-religious-portrait-of-african-americans.

Pew Research Center, 15 June 2011 Living arrangements and father involvement. http://www.pewsocialtrends.org/2011/06/15/chapter-1-living-arrangements-and-father-involvement/

Pew Research Center, 27 September 2018. Black men reverse the gender split on religion, research shows. Retrieved from https://religionnews.com/2018/09/27/black-men-more-religious-than...

Pierce, Y., 8 October 2015. A theology for a grieving people. *Sojourners*. Retrieved from https://sojo.net/articles/how-blacklivesmatter-changed-my-theology/theology-grieving-people.

Pinkney, A., 1993. *Black Americans* (4th ed.). Englewood Cliff: Prentice Hall.

Pinn, A. H. and Pinn, A. B., 2007. *Fortress introduction to Black church history*. Minneapolis: Fortress Press.

Pinsky, M. I., 22 March 2008. Ministers and money (Osteen, Warren, and other rich preachers). *The Orlando Sentinel*. Retrieved from www.freerepublic.com/focus/f-religion/1989864/posts.

Pipes, D., 2002. *Militant Islam reaches America*. New York London: W.W. Norton and Company.

Rainer, T. S., 10 November 2014. Fourteen characteristics of genuinely friendly churches. ThomRainer.com. Retrieved from thomrainer.com/2014/11/...genuinely-friendly-church.

Ranier, T. S., 2015. Nine traits of mean churches. *Charisma News*. Retrieved from http://www.charismanews.com/opinion/48992-9-traits-of-mean-churches

Rees, T. J., 2009. Is personal insecurity a cause of cross-national differences in the intensity of religious belief? *Journal of Religion and Society*, 11, pp. 1-24.

Reinert, D. F. and Edwards, C. E., 2012. Sex differences in religiosity: The role of attachment to parents and social learning. *Pastoral Psychology*, 61, pp. 259-268.

Riley, J. L., 4 November 2012. For Blacks, the pyrrhic victory of the Obama era. Wall Street Journal.

Robins, J., 2010. Allan Anderson, ed. *Studying global Pentecostalism: Theories and methods*. Michael Bergunder, André Droogers, and Cornelis van der Laan. *University of California Press*.

Roth, L. and Kroll, J., 2007. Risky business: Assessing risk-preference explanations for gender differences in religiosity. *American Sociological Review*, 72(2), pp. 205-220.

Ruggles, S., 1994. The origins of African American family structure. *American Sociological Review*, pp. 136–151.

Schmidt, V. H., 2001. Oversocialised epistemology: A critical appraisal of constructivism. *Sociology*, 35(1), pp. 135-157.

Sewell, S., 2001. African American religion: The struggle for community development in a southern city. *Journal of Southern Religion*. Retrieved from http://jsr.as.wvu.edu/2001/jsrlink4.htm.

Sherkat, D., 2002. Sexuality and religious commitment in the United States: An empirical examination. *Journal for the Scientific Study of Religion*, 41, pp. 313–323.

Slavery and the making of America education, arts, and culture. 8 January 2016. Retrieved from www.pbs.org/wnet/slavery/experience/education/history2.html.

Smetana, J. G. and Metzger, A., 2005. Family and religious antecedents of civic involvement in middle class African American late adolescents. *Journal of Research on Adolescence*, 15(3), pp. 325–352.

Smith, J. K. A., 2010. *Thinking in tongues: Pentecostal contributions to Christian philosophy*. William B. Eerdmans Publishing.

Smith, C. and Kim, P., 1997. *Religious Youth Are More Likely to Have Positive Relationships with Their Fathers*. University of North Carolina at Chapel Hill.

Soares, J., 2016. Deprivation theory deprived. *Peace Review*, 18(3) pp. 389-393.

Speller, J., 2005. *Walkin' the talk: Keepin the faith in Afrocentric congregations*. Cleveland: The Pilgrim Press. ISBN 0-8298-1522-8.

Stark, R., 2002. Physiology and faith: Addressing the universal gender difference in religious commitment. *Journal for the Scientific Study of Religion*, 41, pp. 495–507.

Stonestreet, J. and Guthrie, S., 9 May 2017. BreakPoint: Preach Scripture, Fill the Pews. *Break Point*.

Sullins, D. P., 2006. Gender and religion: Deconstructing universality, constructing complexity. *American Journal of Sociology*, 112(3), pp. 838–880.

Swatos, W. H. ed., 1998. African American religious experience. *Encyclopedia of Religion and Society, Hartford Institute for Religion Research*. Retrieved from hirr.hartsem.edu/ency/african.htm.

Taylor, R. J., Thornton, M. C. and Chatters, L. M., 1987. Black Americans' perceptions of the sociohistorical role of the church. *Journal of Black Studies*, 18(2) pp. 123-138. Retrieved from http://www.jstor.org/stable/2784547.

The black church experience, 23 May 2009. Retrieved from theblackchurchexperience.*blogspot.com/...historical*-black-church.*html*.

Thomas, P. A., Krampus, E. M. and Newton, R. R., 19 March 2007. Father presence, family structure, and feelings of closeness to the father among adult African American children. *Journal of Black Studies* 38 (4), pp. 529–546.

Thumma, S. and Travis, D., 2007. *Beyond megachurch myths: What we can learn from America's largest churches*. San Francisco: Jossey-Bass.

U.S. Census Bureau, 2017. *America's families and living*. Retrieved from+ https://census.gov/data/tables/2017/demo/families/cps-2017.html.

Vaidyanathan, B., 2011. Religious resources or differential returns? Early religious socialization and declining attendance in emerging adulthood. *Journal for the Scientific Study of Religion*, 50(2), pp. 366–387.

Van Biema, D., 3 October 2008. Maybe we should blame god for the subprime mess. *Time*. Retrieved from content.time.com/time/business/article/0,8599,1847053,00.html.

van der Ven, J., 1994, 'Empirical methodology in PT. Why and how?' *PTSA*, 9(1), pp. 29-44.

van Rijnsoever, F.J., 2017. (I can't get no) saturation: A simulation and guidelines for sample sizes in qualitative research. *PLoS ONE*, 12 (7), pp. 1-17.

Vermeer, P., Janssen, J. and Scheepers, P., 2012. Authoritative parenting and the transmission of religion in the Netherlands: A panel study. *The International Journal for the Psychology of Religion*, 22, pp. 42–59.

Waller, M., Lissner, L., Hange, D., Sund, V., Blomstrand, A. and Björkelund, C., 2018. Socioeconomic disparities in physical activity among Swedish women and trends over time – the population study of women in Gothenburg. *Scandinavian Journal of Primary Health Care*, 36(4), pp. 363-371.

Walther, C. F. W., 2010. *Law and Gospel: How to Read and Apply the Bible*. Concordia Publishing House.

Walter, T. and Davie, G., 1998. The religiosity of women in the modern west. *British Journal of Sociology*, 49, pp. 640-660.

Warr, M. and Ellison, C., 2000. Rethinking social reactions to crime: Personal and altruistic fear in family households. *American Journal of Sociology*, 106(3), pp. 551-578.

Washington, J., 6 November 2010. Blacks struggle with 72 percent unwed mothers rate. *Boston.com*. Retrieved from archive.boston.com/news/education/higher/articles/2010/11/06/blacks_struggle_with_72_percent_unwed_mothers_rate/.

Weisenfeld, J., March 2015. Cultural history, African American history. Religious History Online. Retrieved from http://americanhistory.oxfordre.com/view/10.1093/acrefore/9780199329175.001.0001/acrefore-9780199329175-e-24.

Wellman, J., 29 July 2013. The importance of good Christian fathers. *Christian Crier*. Retrieved from www.patheos.com/blogs/christiancrier/2013/07/29/the-importance-of-good-christian-fathers/.

West, C. and Glaude, E. S., 2003. *African American religious thought: An anthology*. Louisville: Westminster John Knox Press.

Williams, J. K., 2013. The brotherhood of sleeping car porters. *New York Amsterdam News*, 104(22).

Wilmore, G. S., 1998. *Black religion and Black radicalism: An interpretation of the religious history of African Americans.* Maryknoll, New York: Orbis Books.

Wilson V., 11 May 2017. African American women stand out as working moms play a larger economic role in families. *Economic Policy Institute.* Retrieved from https://www.epi.org/blog/african-american-women-stand-out-as.

Wingfield, H., 1988. The historical and changing role of the Black church: The social and political implication. *The Western Journal of Black Studies*, 12(3).

Woodhead, L., 2005. Gendering secularization theory. *Kvinder, KÃ¸n og Forskning*, 1(1), pp. 187-193.

Wright, J., 2004. *Doing Black theology in the Black church.* In Thomas, Linda E. (ed.), Living Stones in the Household of God. Fortress Press, Minneapolis. ISBN 0-8006-3627-9.

Zoba, W. M., 3 April 2000. Islam, U.S.A. *Christianity Today.*

www.ingramcontent.com/pod-product-compliance
Lightning Source LLC
Chambersburg PA
CBHW071303040426
42444CB00009B/1852